THEOLOGIANS TODAY: HANS KÜNG

THEOLOGIANS TODAY: a series selected and edited
by Martin Redfern

HANS KÜNG

SHEED AND WARD · LONDON AND NEW YORK

First published 1972

Sheed & Ward Inc, 64 University Place, New York, N.Y. 10003
and Sheed & Ward Ltd, 33 Maiden Lane, London WC2E 7LA

This selection © Sheed & Ward Ltd, 1972

Nihil obstat: John M. T. Barton, S.T.D., L.S.S
Imprimatur: ✠ Victor Guazzelli, V.G
Westminster, 20 March 1972

Library of Congress Catalog Number 72-2159

This book is set in 12/14 Monotype Imprint

Made and printed in Great Britain by
Billing & Sons Limited, Guildford and London

CONTENTS

49106

Sources and Acknowledgments

"Justification and Sanctification according to the New Testament" (1959) is from *Christianity Divided*, ed. Daniel J. Callahan and others, New York, Sheed & Ward, 1961; and London, Sheed & Ward, 1962.

"Liturgical Reform and Christian Unity" (1963) is from *The Living Church*, London, Sheed & Ward, 1963; and *The Council in Action*, New York, Sheed & Ward, 1964.

"Freedom in the World" (1964) was first published as *Freedom in the World: St Thomas More*, London, Sheed & Ward, 1965; and in *Freedom Today*, New York, Sheed & Ward, 1966.

"Truthfulness as a Demand of the Message of Jesus" (1968) is from *Truthfulness: the Future of the Church*, London, Sheed & Ward, 1968; and *Truthfulness*, New York, Sheed & Ward, 1969.

INTRODUCTION

The last twenty-five years, and in particular the last ten years, have seen a remarkable flowering of Roman Catholic theology. But for the non-specialist—for the busy parish priest, the active layman, the student—the very wealth of this development presents a range of problems. With which theologian does he begin? Which theologians will he find the most rewarding? Can he ignore any of them?

There are no quick or final answers to such questions, of course, but I hope that this new *Theologians Today* series will help many Catholics to find their own answers more easily. It is designed to achieve two main purposes. Each individual book provides a short but representative introduction to the thought of an outstanding Catholic theologian of the present day, and the series as a whole demonstrates the kind of relationship existing between the best contemporary Catholic theology and official Church teaching.

Both purposes are met by the framework common to all the books. For each book I have selected—and arranged in order of original publication—four pieces which indicate the range in time, approach, and special interest of the theologian concerned. Partly to make my selections more "objective", but mainly to emphasize the close connection between the theologian's writing and the teaching of Vatican II, I have keyed the articles to the four major documents of that Council—the four Constitutions, on the Church, on Revelation, on the Liturgy, and on the Church in the Modern World.

The selections are very much my own. The theologians themselves, or other editors, would doubtless have made different choices. Nevertheless, I feel that—granted my self-imposed limitations of space and conciliar theme, and the further necessary limitations imposed by copyright or by a proper preference for the out-of-print or inaccessible over the widely available—I have done my own best for men to whom I owe a large debt of gratitude.

The four articles in this volume differ widely in style and approach, but several of Hans Küng's most characteristic concerns are evident in more than one of them—the profoundly biblical basis of his dogmatics, his radical ecumenism, his passion for individual freedom, his horror of hypocrisy and cant, his conviction that the whole Church, not just its bishops and theologians, must understand and respond to the call of the Spirit for renewal.

MARTIN REDFERN

1. Justification and Sanctification according the to New Testament

"The Church is concerned to move ahead daily towards a deeper understanding of the Sacred Scriptures so that she may unceasingly feed her sons with the divine words. . . . Catholic exegetes and other students of sacred theology, working diligently together and using appropriate means, should devote their energies, under the watchful care of the sacred teaching office of the Church, to an exploration and exposition of the divine writings."—*Dogmatic Constitution on Divine Revelation*, VI, 23.

Just as there are saints who only seem to be saints and just men who are not really just, so also there is a process of justification which really is not justification, and a process of sanctification which is sanctification in appearance only. Justification and sanctification of sinful man are found in every religion. In some of them it is accomplished through nature magic, in some through pantheistic absorption in the divine, in others through a piety which expresses itself in ritual worship or through a morality which emphasizes active fulfilment of duty. However, what we are speaking of here is not just *any* justification at all or *any* sanctification, and certainly least of all man's autonomous self-justification and self-sanctification, but rather *God's* sanctification and justification of sinful man. In other words, we are speaking of justification and sanctification as they are understood in the Scriptures, which, for the Christian, are binding. It is the Scriptures, God's gracious liberating gift to men, which are the norm not only for what a Christian does, but also for what he says. It is not only "ideas" that Holy Scripture

11

communicates to us, but words freighted with "ideas". An uncommitted "philosophy of religion" may allow itself the liberty of by-passing the biblical words in its search of "ideas"; not so Christian theology, which does not aim at self-interpretation, but at making clear the meaning of the Word of God.

Christian theology will not shun the hard work involved in probing the meaning of the terminology of the Bible, of the words it uses, and the way it uses them. There are a number of different ways of explaining the justification–sanctification relationship. If we want an explanation which comes from the Word of God, we must let ourselves be taught by the terminology of the Bible. Categories which come from outside the Bible need not be eliminated, but the biblical categories must be the standard against which they are checked. Now in the light of Scripture, what is the relationship between justification and sanctification? They must be seen in the unity which underlies their differences.

The New Testament word for justification is the noun *dikaiōsis* with the verb *dikaioun* (to justify), both (together with *dikaiosunē*, or "righteousness") derived from *dikaios* (just, righteous), which in its turn goes back to the root word *dikē* (punishment). The New Testament term for sanctification is the noun *hagiasmos* with the verb *hagiazein* (to sanctify), which stems from *hagios* (holy), as do also *hagiotēs* (holiness) and *hagiosunē* (holiness). If we compare both word groups, we quickly notice that justification and sanctification cannot be separated. It is the same God who is both the Just One (Jn 17:52; 2 Tim 4:8; Rev 16:5) *and* the Holy One (Jn 17:11; 1 Jn 2:20), who justifies (Rom 3:26, 30; 4:5; 8:30,33; Gal 3:8) *and* sanctifies (Jn 17:17; 1 Thess 5:23). It is the same Jesus Christ who is the Holy One *and* the Just One (Acts 3:14), the Just One (Acts 7:25; 22:14; 1 Jn 2:1; 3:7) *and* the Holy One of God (Mk 1:24; Lk 4:34; Jn 6:69), who was justified in the Spirit (1 Tim 3:16) *and* sanctified by the Father (Jn 10:36), in whose name we are justified (1 Cor 6:11; Gal 2:17) *and* sanctified (1 Cor 6:11; 1:2). It is the same Spirit, the Spirit of holiness (Rom 1:4; 2 Thess 2:12), in whom we are justified *and* sanctified (1 Cor 6:11; cf. Rom 15:16).

It is the same redemption in which Christ became our righteousness *and* sanctification (1 Cor 1:30); we were justified (Rom 5:9) *and* sanctified (Heb 10:29; 13:12) in the same blood. By being cleansed in the same baptism, we have been justified *and* sanctified (1 Cor 6:11; Eph 5:26). It is the same Christians who are just (Mt 13:43; Rom 2:13; 5:19; 1 Pet 4:18 and *passim*) *and* holy (Acts 9:13,32; Rom 8:27; 12:13; 15:25 and *passim*), who are the justified (Rom 3:24) *and* the sanctified (Heb 10:14; Acts 20:32; 26:18), and who nevertheless actively await justification (Gal 5:5) *and* sanctification (Rom 6:22; 1 Thess 4:3).

Whoever would tear justification and sanctification one from the other does not let the Scriptures teach him, but rather makes up his own teaching. The same theocentricity prevails in both justification and sanctification. It is the just and holy Father *alone* who justifies and sanctifies: "It is God who justifies" (Rom 8:33). "May the God of peace himself sanctify you through and through" (1 Thess 5:23). And the same Christocentricity likewise prevails in both: *Only* in Jesus Christ who is *the* Just One and *the* Holy One does the justification and sanctification of sinful men take place directly and primordially. "Jesus Christ, who was our righteousness and sanctification" (1 Cor 1:30). As in justification, so also in sanctification it is *man* who is being genuinely affected by the justifying and sanctifying action of God. Man receives through the Holy Spirit a real share in the justification and sanctification of Christ and is changed in his very being. "Now you *have* been sanctified, now you *have* been justified through the name of the Lord Jesus Christ and through the Spirit of our God" (1 Cor 6:11).

In both justification *and* sanctification the movement proceeds from above downwards, from the Father who is the *solus sanctus* (the only Holy One) and *solus justus* (the only Just One), through his crucified and risen Son Jesus Christ, who is one with him in the Holy Spirit, to the man who is to be justified and sanctified. Not only justification but sanctification as well is rooted in God's eternal decree: "From the beginning God has chosen you for salvation in sanctification through the Spirit" (2 Thess 2:12). "Thus has he truly chosen us in him (Christ) from the foundation of the world, so that we might be holy and blameless before him" (Eph 1:4). Sanctification is not simply—as has often been asserted—the human counter-movement from below, the responsive action of men in sanctification answering to the divine action of justification. No, the origin and beginning of justification and sanctification are from above, in the action of God. The centre and the basis of justification *and* sanctification are in Jesus Christ. The power and the seal of justification *and* sanctification is the Holy Spirit of Jesus Christ, and of the Father, through whom justification *and* sanctification develop and reach their goal in individual men. Man *receives* justification *and* sanctification. Whereas a *justification* from below, coming from men, appears at least as a possibility in the purview of the New Testament, a *sanctification* which would take its beginning from below appears to be ruled out from the start. That sanctification can take place only from above downwards is, for the New Testament, an evident presupposition which does not even need to be argumentatively established. All sanctification in the New Testament proceeds from God. That the Temple (Mt 23:17), the altar (Mt 23:19), and the sacrifice (Heb 9:13) are able to sanctify, are able to possess sanctifying power, all this presupposes the holiness of God. Just as the kingdom of God comes (in men) through God himself, just as the will of God is done (in men) through God himself, so also the name of God is sanctified (in men) through God himself (Mt 6:9; Lk 11:2). It is not merely a benediction but a genuine

15

request to our Father: May he himself reveal his holiness. God himself—in cautious passive paraphrase—is the logical subject of sanctification (cf. Ezek 36:23; 20:41; 28:22; 38:16; Is 5:16). And the divinity of Jesus Christ becomes manifest in the fact that he—sanctified by the Father (Jn 10:36)—sanctifies himself (Jn 17:19), and then also his disciples (Jn 17:19) and the Church (Eph 5:26; Heb 2:11; 10:10,14; 13:12). It is not without cause that the concept of sanctification is St Paul is employed mainly in the passive sense: the sanctified in Jesus Christ (1 Cor 1:2), in the Holy Spirit (Rom 15:16), those *called* by God to be saints (1 Cor 1:2; Rom 1:7). Christians can and ought to sanctify Christ in their hearts (1 Pet 3:15), *because* they themselves are saints through God (1 Pet 1:15 f.). So, in contradistinction to other religions, it is God's sanctifying will and Word which stand altogether in the foreground. *He* sanctifies his people and sanctifies individuals; *he* brings his claim upon the whole of life. In view of this work of God, only this can be said about the work of man: "As he who has called you is holy, you also ought to be holy in all your dealings, for it is written: 'Be holy, *for I* am holy' " (1 Pet 1:15 f.; cf. Lev 11:44). The phrase "sanctification of man" is speaking more of the production of this sanctification by God in man than of man's possession of this sanctification. The Father sanctifies the Son (Jn 10:36) and the Son sanctifies himself (Jn 17:19) so that men may be sanctified (Jn 17:19) in him who is the "holy one of God" in the absolute sense, that is, in him who as the sanctifier produces those who are sanctified (Heb 2:11).

Justification and sanctification belong together, form a unity in the single event of salvation in Jesus Christ. This dies not mean that justification and sanctification may be confused. A theological reduction of these two concepts to one would not correspond to exegetical findings; it would pass over the contrasts which are fruitful precisely for theological reflection, and it would lead eventually to a very dangerous distortion of the Christian message.

1. *Justification has a legal character*

The root word for *dikaioun* (to justify) and *dikaiōsis* (justification) is *dikē* (punishment), which occurs only three times in the New Testament and is always understood as criminal justice and punishment (Acts 28:4; 2 Thess 1:9; Jude 7). Whatever its etymology may be, it is a basic concept of the *legal* sphere. This holds good especially for the Greek of the classical and Hellenist periods. The enormous theological significance of the idea of justice in the Old Testament is well known. Consider in the present context the importance of the legal trial as the typical image of God's dealings with the just and unjust men.

But even the verb form *dikaioun* (to justify) is no less obviously legal in character. In this all lines which lead to the New Testament word agree: the Old Testament *sdq* means a "court pronouncement of justification" (which is of the highest importance precisely for Pauline terminology because of its general dependence on Old Testament terminology). In classical Greek also, in Hellenism, and in the Septuagint (which Paul cites), *dikaioun* (to justify) is a legal concept. Especially significant, finally, is the legal aspect of justification in the synagogue teaching, with which Paul had to carry on controversy. In all his other attacks, this aspect is never placed in question. For his own terminology he has drawn extensively upon the juridical language of the Pharisees.

And thus in New Testament usage as well the legal keynote of *dikaioun* (to justify) is unmistakable. Though not everywhere emphasized, nevertheless, it is operative throughout. And even if it is not apodictically provable in every text, its presence can still be easily detected. It is certainly clear in the Synoptics: Mt 11:19 (cf. Rom 3:4); Mt 12:37; Lk 10:29; 16:15; 18:14. Clear traces of this legal emphasis are to be found especially in Paul in the eschatological texts (Rom 2:13; 8:33; 1 Cor 4:4): *dikaioun* (to justify) can be understood only in the legal sense. It is probable that with the passage of time "to justify" was used by the Jews in an eschatological sense, and that as a result of this, legal-eschatological justice in Paul is already attributed to man in the present time. He especially is considered as "justified" who is pronounced free in a legal process (in the *krinesthai*, "going to law"), who has won (in Rom 3:4 *dikaiōthēnai*, "to be justified", and *nikan*, "to win", are placed in parallel). That is, generally speaking, the innocent party, but not insofar as he *is* innocent but insofar as he is *recognized* as such. In Jesus Christ to be sure—the paradox of grace (Rom 3:23 f.; 5:20)—it is precisely the unjust one who is recognized as just on the basis of his faith, and thus "to justify" now means the same as "to reckon faith as righteousness" (Rom 4; Gal 3:6).

For the legal usage of *dikaioun* "to justify) this is likewise the case. The *enōpion autou* (in his sight: Rom 3:20) and *para tō theō* (before God: Gal 3:11; Rom 2:13) used with this word are characteristic court forms. The opposite of *dikaioun* (to justify), that is *katakrinein* (to condemn: Rom 8:34; 1 Cor 4:3–6), is a legal concept. Also the use of *dikaiōsis* (justification) and *dikaiōma* (justification) (precisely in contrast to *katakrima*, "condemnation") is legal. The adjective *dikaios* (just) manifests even in the Septuagint a strong connection with the judgment of God. Man is just when he is recognized as such, that is, when he is declared just or is justified, if this was necessary. Finally, the noun *dikaiosunē* (righteousness) goes considerably beyond the meaning of *dikaioun* (to justify), yet the legal traces are unmistakable even here. These traces are recognizable not only in the Greek moral teaching in Josephus and Philo, not only in the Old Testament, in the Septuagint and the synagogue, but also in the New Testament itself, both in the non-Pauline and especially in the Pauline writings. *Dikaiosunē* (righteousness) as a condition of salvation or also as a fruit of salvation is possessed by man not simply in himself but in the presence of another to whom he is answerable, in the judgment of another who attributes it to him (not as a quality but as a relationship). Nonetheless, precisely in the case of *dikaiosunē*, "righteousness" (and also with the adjective *dikaios*, "just") as the union of judgment and *grace*, it becomes particularly clear that in "the act of justifying" (*dikaioun*) and in "justification" there is no question of an act where the judge makes good a debt, but one in which the judge bestows unmerited grace for the salvation of man. The grace-character of justification, in which precisely the *un*just person is acquitted and declared just, shows that *God's* justification can be conceived only analogously as a legal act.

Dikaioun is thus used by Paul almost exclusively for God's judgment, either for the act of God which justifies or for man's acquittal by which he is changed into a *dikaios* (just man) and receives in Christ the divine gift of *dikaiosunē* (righteousness).

The legal character is of fundamental significance for justification. Since it is a question not merely of some physical occurrence in man but of a statement that he is just, a declaration of justice, a court judgment, a nonreckoning of sins, and a reckoning of Christ's justice (imputation: Rom 4; Gal 3:6) through *God*—for that reason the *gravity* of the situation, in contrast to all sinful frivolity, becomes evident: what is involved is *God*, his personal anger, and his personal grace. But precisely for that reason, in opposition to all the faintheartedness and despair of the tormented conscience, the overriding *consolation* of the situation is manifest. It is not I myself who must strive in vain to cast off my burden of guilt. No, it is God himself who lifts it off because he forgives me, whole and entire, through his gracious word. Catholic tradition not only does not exclude the legal character of justification, but actually includes it. Catholic tradition, however, lays great stress on this: God's justification must be taken seriously; God does what he says. When God declares a man just, he draws him into the righteousness of God and thus he effects a transformation of man's very being. When God *says* a man is just, since it is *God* who says it, man is simultaneously *made* just. From this it follows that justification includes in itself all the effects which touch the very being of the man who is justified, and his effective transformation, and thus also includes a positive sanctification effected by God. But it remains true that biblical and especially the Pauline act of justifying ("justification") does not say this explicitly.

2. Sanctification is linked to divine worship

The stern word *hagios* (holy) is originally a concept connected with worship and is used in speaking of the characteristics of persons and things that are allowed to come into contact with God. It is used in nonbiblical Greek first of all in connection with the sanctuary and takes on an Oriental colouring in the Hellenistic period. It conveys all the inflections of its Hebraic equivalent *qdš*. This in its turn has from the very beginning onward, in noun, adjectival, and verb forms, an intimate connection with the divine worship, whether it is used in speaking of God, man, things, or time. *qdš*, (*hagios*, holy), the basic concept of worship, is in actual fact cognate with *thr* (purity, *hagnos*), which is the basic concept of ritual. But both of them have their origin not on the level of human morality but on the level of the divinely numinous. Only in the course of time, in the theology of the prophets, does the concept of worship-sanctification gradually change into the moral concept, so that in postexilic Judaism the stream emphasizing priesthood and worship (predominant in the literature of the Law) joins the stream which stresses prophecy and morality (prevalent in the Psalm poetry). Yet in the postexilic literature, as also later in the rabbinical, the concept of *hagios* (holy) never loses its connection with its origins in a context of worship.

The New Testament concept of holiness rests on that of the Old Testament. The connection between holiness and worship is already expressed in the name of God (Rev 4:8). Although the holiness of the Father is more presupposed than expressed, the deutero–Isaian expression *ho hagios pais* (the holy servant), *'bd yhwh* (the servant of Yahweh), is applied to Christ (Acts 4:27,30; cf. Mt 12:18). This, an expression simultaneously of loftiness and lowliness, points—always with an indication of divine origin—

to the role destined for the saviour in divine worship. Christ offers himself as a holy victim in order to reopen to the sinful people the entrance to the sanctuary (intimated in Acts 3:14; 4:27; then above all in 1 Pet 1:18; Heb 9). Christ appears simultaneously as victim, priest, and temple. But it is in the Holy Spirit of Jesus that the new community of worship is founded (Rom 5:5; 1 Cor 3:16; 6:19; 2 Cor 13:13; Eph 2:20–22). He dwells in the Christian community (1 Thess 4:8; 2 Tim 1:14) to the degree that it exists in the sanctification of the Spirit (2 Thess 2:13). The holy people is a royal priesthood (1 Pet 2:9), and at the same time a victim sanctified in the Holy Spirit (Rom 15:16), the holy and faultless Church (Eph 5:27), the Church of the saints (1 Cor 14:33). Yet in relation to individual Christians, too, the connection between holiness and worship is obvious; the Christian life as a holy sacrifice wellpleasing to God (Rom 12:1; 15:16), holy and blameless (*amōmos*, "without blemish", in the sense of faultlessness for worship or suitability for the rite of worship). Especially pronounced is the worship character of *hagios* (holy) in its application to the flesh of the victim (Mt 7:6), to the sanctuary (Heb 8:2; 9:1,2,3,24,25; 13:11), to Jerusalem (Mt 4:5; 27:53; Acts 11:2; 21:12; 22:18), to the Temple (Mt 24:15; Acts 6:13; 21:28), to the convenant (Lk 1:72), to the Scriptures (Rom 1:2), to the kiss (Rom 16:16; 1 Cor 16:20; 2 Cor 13:12). The theme of worship which is associated with the concept of *hagios* (holy) is discernible throughout all of the

23

Old and New Testament up to and including their eschatology (Rev 20:6; 22:11).

But what about the words which are used not just to say "holy" or "holiness" (*hagiotēs, hagiosunē*) but to express directly the idea of "sanctification"? *Hagiazein* (to sanctify) which occurs almost exclusively in biblical Greek, already in the Septuagint, as a translation of *qdš*, has a meaning linked to worship. In the New Testament it is used for things which are dedicated to use in worship or which render things suitable for worship (Mt 23:17,19; 1 Tim 4:5), or for persons upon whom a special fitness for worship was conferred, who, having been drawn into the holy sphere, and for that reason consecrated, are made holy. This happens through Baptism (1 Cor 6:11; Eph 5:26), through the blood of sacrifice (Heb 9:13), through the blood of Christ (Heb 13:12; cf. 2:11; 10:10), through contact with some holy person (1 Cor 7:14). The undercurrent of emphasis on worship is therefore especially tangible in the connection of sanctification with the propitiation sacrifice (Heb 2:14; 10:10,14,29; 13:12; Rom 15:15), with purity (Eph 1:4; 5:26; Col 1:22; 1 Tim 4:5; 2 Tim 2:21), and with Baptism (1 Cor 6:11; Eph 5:26). Only with the word *hagiasmos* (consecration), which in contrast to the words *hagiotes* (holiness as the state of being holy: 2 Cor 1:12; Heb 12:10) and *hagiosunē* (holiness as a dynamic, active property: Rom 1:4; 2 Cor 7:1; 1 Thess 3:13; it has its origin in propitiation and thus has an element of worship), means not holiness but sanctification, and that in the active sense, is the stress now clearly placed on the moral element: the exercise of holiness especially through putting aside impurity (*akatharsia*): Rom 6:19,22; 1 Thess 4:3,4,7; 2 Thess 2:13; 1 Tim 2:15; Heb 12:14.

From the original connection of sanctification with ritual worship it becomes clear that the biblical concept of sanctification has a *Sitz in Leben* (life context) different from that of the concept of justification. Here the picture of a trial and judgment never stands in the background. But *qdš* is used to indicate segregation and cutting off, separation and setting apart from all that is profane and impure, being especially chosen for God's service; the pure becomes the holy by being withdrawn from profane use and consecrated by a positive act to God. In the New Testament the physical element in sanctification drops out (Jerusalem, Temple, holy of holies, sacrificial gifts, times of worship, instruments of worship, vestments of worship etc.: what is alluded to in the New Testament is spoken of in the perspective of the Old Testament), that is, it becomes transformed into something spiritual. (Cf., for example, Rom 12:1 f. where the religious terminology of ritual worship is given a spiritual and ethical meaning.) Sanctification is the action of God which sets life in opposition to sin and lays claim to it for himself: a separation from what is worldly and sinful and a special election for what is divine and sacred. So, according to the New Testament, holiness in the context of ritual worship consists in being snatched

25

out of this world of sin, of darkness and of Satan (Acts 26:18; Eph 2:19; Col 1:12 f.), and consequently in being called to share in the heritage of the saints (Eph 1:18; Col 1:12; 2 Thess 2:13; 1 Pet 1:15). At the same time, this concept of holiness receives a transcendental character and expresses the divine elevation of God above the world, which the saints can share (cf. the expression *pneuma hagion* [holy spirit] as the spirit which goes out from God, or *graphai hagiai* [holy writings] as the writings which are produced by God, or the implantation of believers into divine truth described in Jn 17).

We saw that sanctification is always tied in with justification. We shall go on to see in what way the two are linked. But just as the declaration of justice in the Bible does not explicitly include sanctification, neither does sanctification in the Bible explicitly include declaration of justice.

3. *Justification is directed more to the individual, sanctification to the group*

Even justification is not purely a personal affair of individuals, but it is a concern of the community. Paul himself does not isolate justification as a private event but places it within the over-all salvation-history context of the redemption of *all* men for the Church (Rom 5:18 f.; cf. 5:12–17; 8:32; 11:32; 2 Cor 5:14; 1 Tim 2:6). In Christ's death and Resurrection all are redeemed and justified (Rom 3:21–26; 4:25; 5:9; 8:3; Gal 3:13; 2 Cor 5:18–21; cf. Jn 12:31). The collective, ecclesiological character of justification cannot be overlooked and every individualistic doctrine of justification is a false approach (the questions of the theology of the Church and the sacraments related to the doctrine of justification are excluded from our treatment here).

And yet it is true that justification—in contrast to sanctification—is directed more to the individual (who of course then becomes at once a member of the body of Christ). It is striking that neither *dikaioun* (to justify) nor *dikaiōsis* (justification) is ever met in connection with *ekklēsia* (church) or a corresponding word. A similar observation can be made with regard to the use of *dikaios* (just) and *dikaiosunē* (righteousness). In general, the way community relationships are pushed into the background when dealing with justification is striking, as contrasted with the way sanctification is treated.

When we consider the legal character of justification, this observation is not surprising. It is a matter of God's personal declaration of justice, and so it is definitely the *individual* who is put on trial. It is a matter of God's personal judgment, before which the individual must take a stand, i.e., must submit himself in faith. For this reason the most "objective" statements about God's justice are always the very ones which are linked to faith (cf. Rom 1:17; 3:22,28; 4; 5:1). If faith is to be reckoned as justice (Rom 4:3, 5 f.; 9:11-22; Gal 3:6), then this affair is a matter of personal reckoning for each individual. Hence justification, precisely because of its legal character, though certainly not individualistic, is still determi-

27

ned primarily on an individual basis.

It is different in the case of sanctification. Naturally the New Testament speaks about individual "saints" (prophets in Lk 1:70; Acts 2:21; 2 Pet 3:2; John the Baptist in Mk 6:20; the Apostles in Eph 3:5; Christians in 1 Pet 1:16 and *passim*; cf. the expression *hoi hagioi*, "the saints", in Acts 9:13,32; Rom 8:27 and *passim*). How could there be a holy body without holy members? (Eph 4 and *passim*). The individual personal character of sanctification is unmistakable and every collectivistic doctrine of sanctification a false approach.

But the holy members are always seen as a part of the holy community. And it is the idea of ritual worship which makes clear why in sanctification the community aspect stands in the foreground. For a new holy generation has sprung up, a royal priesthood, a holy people (1 Pet 2:9). Christ, the Holy One of God, is the founder of the new worship community. He has sacrificed himself for his Church in order to sanctify it, so that it might be holy and blameless (Eph 5:26 f.). Thus this community has been founded by his death (Rom 5:9 ff.; 2 Cor 5:18 f.); its visible signs are Baptism (Rom 6:3; 1 Cor 12:13; Col 2:12; Titus 3:5), and the Lord's Supper (1 Cor 11:26; 12:13; 2 Cor 5:17). National boundaries are torn down. God's people are no longer only the Israelites but Gentiles as well. They also are God's holy and beloved chosen ones (Col 3:11). They are those sanctified in Christ Jesus (1 Cor 1:2; cf. 6:11), a sacrificial gift, sanctified in the Holy Spirit (Rom 15:16), no more foreigners or strangers, but fellow citizens of the saints and members of God's household (Eph 2:19), made capable of sharing in the inheritance of the saints in light (Col 1:12), in the riches of his glorious heritage in the community of the saints (Eph 1:18). In this way Jew and Gentile—both communities are often designated as the "saints"—form a holy and spotless Church (Eph 5:27) into which the individual churches of the saints (1 Cor 14:33) are incorporated as participating communities. A holy temple in which the believers are the living stones and in which God dwells in the Spirit (Eph 2:21; cf. 1 Cor 3:16; 6:19; Eph 2:20), a community of the Holy Spirit (Rom 5:5; 2 Cor 13:13; 1 Thess 4:8; 2 Tim 1:14), in which Christ himself is priest and victim (Heb 9). Accordingly, Paul views the Christian community of the "saints" (Rom 1:7; 1 Cor 1:2; 14:33; 2 Cor 1:1; Eph 1:1; Phil 1:1; Col 1:2 and *passim*), as a people (Rom 9:25 f.; 11:1 f.; 15:10; 2 Cor 6:16), as Israel (Rom 9:8; Gal 3:29; 4:26 ff.; 6:16; Phil 3:3), as *ekklēsia* or "church" (1 Cor 1:2; Eph 1:22; 5:23; Col 1:18 and *passim*), as temple (1 Cor 3:16 f.; 2 Cor 6:16; Eph 2:21), as body (1 Cor 10:16 f.; 12:12 ff.; Eph 1:23 f.; 4:4,12,16; Col 1:18; 3:15 and *passim*), as bride (2 Cor 11:2; Eph 5:26 f.).

Thus in the New Testament and especially with Paul the Christians are regarded as a collectivity, as the continuation of the chosen, holy people of God in the Old Covenant, that is to say, as *ekklēsia* or "church", as the assembly of those summoned

29

through God to holiness, to a participation in his own holiness. The Christian community is holy—not through itself, but through the Spirit who is the sanctifier. The individual Christian is holy in the Holy Spirit (Baptism) through his membership in the holy community. Because he belongs to the holy community, he is set apart from the world and sin, and chosen out for God.

Hence sanctification, precisely because of its worship charter, derives its characteristics from a situation which, though not "collectivistic," is nevertheless predominantly collective.

4. *No self-justification*

From the fundamentally legal character of justification a further conclusion naturally follows. It is not works, not normal achievements which count in justification. "We hold that man is justified through faith (alone) without the works of the law" (Rom 3:28). "Only for him who does not perform works, but rather believes in him who justifies the godless, will faith be reckoned as justice" (Rom 4:5). "But since we know that no man is justified by works of the law but through faith in Jesus Christ, we also have believed in Christ Jesus in order to be justified by faith in Christ, and not by the works of the law, because by works of the law no man is justified" (Gal 2:15–16; cf. 3:5–14,24; 5:5; Rom 3:21–28; 4; 5:11; 9:30–32; 10:4–6; 1 Cor 4:7; 2 Cor 12:9; Phil 3:9).

Looking at the problem as he does from an anti-

Pharisaical viewpoint, Paul is referring primarily to the works of the Mosaic law, but all other works and moral achievements of man are included. If even the works prescribed by the holy law of Israel do not contribute to justification, then a fortiori other works certainly do not. For it is certainly not true that the works of the law would be evil *in themselves;* certainly they must also be fulfilled by the *believer*, in a new way of course, through love (Rom 3:31; 13:8; Gal 5:14). What is false in the old way is that works, with a view to justification, wanted to provide grounds for man's *kaukhasthai* (glorying). Since works want to be somehow one's own achievement, which could mean "glory" for man, they are *for this very reason* radically useless for justification (Rom 3:2 f.). And this is true not only for the works of the Jews whose sinful basic attitude is actually "self-glorification" (Rom 2:17,23), but also for the works of the Gentiles (1 Cor 1:19–31). *No one* may glory before God (1 Cor 1:29) except in the Lord (1 Cor 1:31; 2 Cor 10:17) and in his own frailty (2 Cor 11:30; 12:9; Gal 6:14). Should man praise himself for *any* of his works, he would be forgetting that he has *nothing* which he has not *received* (1 Cor 1:29). Every justice "of one's own" is to be ruled out (Rom 10:3). Whether it be works of the Mosaic law, whether it be works of general morality—they avail not at all for the justification of man. No one can stand before God in his own strength. We are justified through God's *grace*, and thereby *every* human achievement is excluded when justification

31

is in question (Rom 3:24; 4:14–16; 5:13,17; 6:14; 11:5 f.; Gal 2:21; 5:4). "But if it is by grace, then it is no longer on the basis of works; otherwise grace would no longer be grace" (Rom 11:6). If by grace, then it will be impossible to speak of a justification given because of *any* obligation.

Every human work, every human achievement, is excluded, but not every human *act*, which does not set itself up as the achievement of some work but rather as renunciation of achievement, which does not desire to force itself through by works, but rather trustfully to abandon itself. This fundamental deed of man, which is supremely active in its extreme passivity, is *faith*. Faith is the radical surrender of *kaukhēsis*, of "glorying" (Rom 3:27). This faith, which it at the same time radical obedience (Rom 1:5; Gal 3:2,5), is not justification itself. It is, however, the condition for the subjective reception and for the realization of justification in man (Rom 1:17; 3:22,26,28,30; 4; 5:1; 9:30,32; 10:6,10; Gal 2:16; 3:6–14,24–27; 5:5; Phil 3:9).

Justification through "faith alone" bespeaks the complete incapacity and incompetence of man for any sort of self-justification. In justification the sinner cannot give anything which he does not receive from grace. The attitude of simple trusting submission under God's gracious judgment is faith, which does not even appeal to its own self, its deed or its attitude, which would only be the craftiest kind of "glorying" (1 Cor 4:7; Rom 4:20). Thus, no work, not even a work of love, justifies man, but only faith,

32

justified through God himself. This faith as a gracious gift of God is not achievement through works, but rather self-surrender to God, an abandonment by grace to the grace of God as a response to the act of God. This basic human act as a reception of the kerygma is simultaneously insight (Rom 5:3; 6:8 f.; 2 Cor 1:7; 4:13 f.; 5:6) and trust (Gal 3:6; 4:3; 2 Cor 1:9); it is simultaneously recognition, acknowledgment and profession of faith, and includes fear (Rom 11:20–25; 2 Cor 5:11) as well as hope (Rom 4:18; 5:5).

And love? There are works of love, but they too are excluded from justification, although the belief of the justified man must be active in love (Gal 5:6). Still, love itself is not a work. Insofar as it too looks away from itself and surrenders itself unconditionally and entirely to God, it is rather to be classified as faith. There is a dead faith of the demons, which yields only knowledge and not self-surrender (Jas 2:19). Yet this is not the genuine, loving faith for which God justifies the sinner. Faith and love, if they are genuine, are a surrender of the whole man. There is no genuine faith without love, no genuine love without faith. However, in faith the dominant element is trusting (and, of course, loving) self-submission in view of one's own worthlessness; while in love, what dominates is self-forgetting (and, of course, believing) self-effacement in the contemplation of God's lovableness. But neither lives without the other, and each lives from and in the other. It is not without reason that faith and love are

B

named to describe the whole of Christian existence together with hope which expresses the eschatological tension contained in man's gift of himself (1 Cor 13:13; 1 Thess 1:3; 5:8). Without love, faith would be nothing (1 Cor 13:2). Genuine love is rooted in faith, just as true faith culminates in love. Faith is made living through love, for love is the gift of the Spirit of life. We are thus not surprised that in the broader context of justification (Rom 5:1), love also is still spoken of, the love of God, that is, which is poured out in our hearts through the Holy Spirit who has been given to us (Rom 5:5). Through the Spirit the love of God in us becomes the new power of life, so that we ourselves are capable of perfecting faith in love (1 Cor 13:13). So also in justification, faith is not present without love in which it is always God, of course, who justifies, and not either faith or love.

But what is the reason, after all, for the correlation of justification and *faith* which Sacred Scripture clearly intends? Even in Rom 5:5 there is no *direct* connection between justification and love, quite apart from the fact that in that text there is question not of the love of man but of the love of God. And the different interpretations of the exegetes leave it quite uncertain whether Luke 7:47 (cf. also 1 Pet 4:8) treats of justification in the strict sense. Why then does Sacred Scripture never speak about justification by love and always speaks emphatically about justification by faith? This too is understandable if we think with the legal character of justification in mind.

34

Justification and Sanctification

Justification is the declaration of justice by God in a court judgment, and the appropriate human attitude is obedient submission to this judgment. Justification is the declaration of justice by the *merciful judge*, and the human attitude appropriate to this is one supported by fear and above all by trust, the abandonment which affirms one's own unworthiness before God's grace under the divine judgment of grace. In short: faith. Certainly a faith of one who loves, and thus a loving faith, yet not a love which overshadows faith. It is not in accordance with the situation of the sinner for him to forget his sinfulness and to lose himself in God's gracious lovableness without regard for his own pitiable state of sinfulness. Faith in and from love certainly, but—for the sinner who is still to be justified—a love which is bashful, not bold. It would be impudent love if the prodigal son. unmindful of his state, simply fell upon his father's neck with the words: "I love you"; instead of—in confused love—casting himself down before him and humbly, trustingly confessing: "Father, I have sinned; I no longer deserve to be called your son." It would be impudent love if the sinful woman, forgetting her past, presumed lightheartedly to be an intimate friend of the merciful Lord, instead of—in ashamed love—with tears for her sins, kissing his feet from behind in order to beg his mercy. It would be impudent love if the sinner with embarrassing misjudgment of the situation should speak of love, instead of—in ashamed love—accepting in simple faith the merciful forgiveness of God. As if it were not precisely the love of God of which the sinner had shown himself unworthy, and thus would first of all have to confess that he was no longer worthy to love the Father, in order once again to *become* worthy of love. As if justification were the trivial reconciliation of two lovers who had fallen out and would only have to throw themselves in one another's arms to be able to sing: "And everything is fine again, everything!" As if justification were a loving "reciprocity" on the same level and not rather the merciful *judgment of God upon* the sinner! Confronted with this judgment, what is appropriate is not an avowal of love, but—precisely because it is love ashamed of itself—a confident submission in faith. Thus although faith without love is worth nothing, Sacred Scripture always with good reason speaks of justification through faith. This faith, however, which excludes all works and merits for justification itself, desires, once justified, to co-operate actively through works of love; a faith which proves itself efficacious through love (Gal 5:6).

It was Paul who occupied himself expressly with the question of the "how" of becoming just. Now it is characteristic that in the specifically Pauline usage of *dikaioun* (to justify), he never speaks of self-justification by men. *Dikaioun* (to justify) is used either in speaking of God, who himself justifies (Rom 3:26,30; 4:5; 8:30,33; Gal 3:8), or of man who does not justify but is *justified* (Rom 2:13; 3:20,24–28; 4:2; 5:1,9; 1 Cor 4:4; 6:11; Gal 2:16 f.;

3:11,24; 5:4; Ti 3:7). Some instances to be added from the rest of the New Testament, also applied to men in the passive sense, are: Mt 12:37; Lk 18:14; Acts 13:39; Rev 22:11 (the unconditionally preferred reading is, however: *dikaiosunēn poiēsato eti*: the just man ought to continue to advance in the practice of justice); Rom 6:7; and Acts 13:38 (*dikaiōthēnai apo*: pronounced free of guilt or sins). Neither do the following texts express self-justification: Rom 3:4 (so that your justice may be vindicated: said of God), 1 Tim 3:16 (proven just in the Spirit: said of Christ), Mt 11:19 (wisdom is proven just; cf. Lk 7:35), Lk 7:29 (to acknowledge God's justice). Only two texts in Luke speak of a self-justification. In Lk 10:29 the question at issue is not justification in the theological sense, but self-justification in human conversation. Lk 16:15 on the contrary has theological import. The Pharisees want to declare themselves as just before men, to represent themselves as just. This is rejected decisively by Jesus with an appeal to God's judgment.

Nor does James speak of self-justification. He always uses *dikaioun* (to justify) passively with reference to man. Man *is* justified by God, which James presupposes as completely obvious. To be sure, this is on the basis of works, as James declares, in explicit opposition to the Pauline thesis (Jas 2:14–26). Yet we observe a fundamentally different *Problematik*. Both ask themselves: how does man become just? Paul, however, in his answer is arguing vigorously against Pharisaical self-righteousness,

James against lazy, literal orthodoxy. For this reason Paul maintains: it is not man with his works who justifies, but God by faith. But James says: only then is a man just if his faith bears fruits in works. Yet, although Paul with his "by faith alone" has no intention of defending Corinthian libertinism, James with his "faith and works" is no less opposed to Pharisaical merit morality. Paul has no more intention of substituting faith for works than James has of substituting works for faith. Nonetheless, Paul's posing of the question is more comprehensive: he too emphasizes the necessity of works (which for him represent fruits of the Spirit, and by which man is judged). Yet, whereas James directs his polemic only against lazy faith-quietism and thus remains more on the surface, Paul simultaneously proceeds against the empty activism of work and poses the question of justification on another level. Paul penetrates thereby into that ultimate depth where even every good work of man is questioned— through the grace of Christ, which strikes the sinner. In this last depth of the grace of God which justifies the sinner, only one thing is appropriate for sinful man: faith which trustfully accepts it. Thus Paul's "through faith alone" constitutes the presupposition for James' (and Paul's) "faith and works" (works as the fruits of the Holy Spirit). One easily perceives that the same thing means something different in Paul and James, respectively: "justice": the ethical agreement of doctrine and life (James), and the gift of God's grace freely promised to the sinner (Paul); "faith": the merely intellectual advertence to a fact, which in itself is dead (James), and the assenting, self-giving of the whole man, confidently ratifying the kerygma, made active in love (Paul); "works": works of piety and love of the neighbour to be practised by the Christian (James), and works of the law or of general morality preceding justification (Paul). Thus "justification" is taken by James not in the strict sense of Paul, but in a wider sense. The verbal contradictions in this instance are not real contradictions. Difficult as it is to establish an agreement between Paul and James, in any event self-justification is out of the question in James as well.

Thus only once (Lk 16:15) does the New Testament employ *dikaioun* (to justify) for self-justification —in order to reject it sharply. Likewise the term *dikaiōsis* (justification) is never used for a self-justification. In the New Testament, of course, God's justification of sinners means the self-justification of *God* (Rom 3:26), but no way leads from God's justification to the self-justification of *man*.

Certainly the justified sinner has become just and ought to live as a just person, ought to seek righteousness, ought to practise righteousness (Rev 22:11). "Righteousness" operates directly in life, is related to action, more than holiness which—according to the meaning of the word—signifies primarily an enduring condition of consecration to God. But it is not by practising and seeking after righteousness that man justifies himself. Neither before nor after

39

God's justification ought he to justify himself, not is he able to do so. Once again this is connected with the legal character of justification. The sinner is pronounced just, and he ought to submit himself in faith to this judgment. It is not up to him to pass a sentence in his own case to his own advantage. As a sinner in need of justification, he is completely and wholly unqualified to do that. But this is true even *after* God's justifying judgment. Without any merit of man, indeed, contrary to his whole sinful being, this judgment becomes an acquittal which brings salvation. Justification purely from the grace of God! How then could he who has been graciously judged and justified by God subsequently dare to set himself up as a self-justifying judge? As if grace does not *remain* just that—grace!

From the legal nature of justification, we understand why Paul nowhere derives a moral demand from the juridical doctrine itself of justification. Even where it would seem to suggest itself naturally, namely, in the midst of his explanation of the doctrine of justification where he has to answer the libertarian objection, his ethical argument is not based directly on the justifying judgment of God, but on Baptism and burial in Christ (Rom 6:1 ff.). It is not as if the doctrine of justification could be isolated. This was emphasized and will be re-emphasized immediately. Yet, in order not falsely to turn God's work of grace into a grace merited by man's works, it must be asserted with great vigour that God's justification of the sinner may not be allowed to become the self-justification of the sinner.

5. *But "self-justification"*

Now with sanctification the case is different. God's sanctification impels man to sanctify his own self. "Just as he who calls you is holy, so also ought you to become holy in all your dealings. For it is written: 'Be holy, for I am holy'" (1 Pet 1:15 f.; cf. Lev 11:44). This "self-sanctifying" of man can be very easily misunderstood. It is God who sanctifies; we saw that. God in Jesus Christ. On the Cross, the Holy One of God, rejected by man, sacrificed himself for our sanctification, to be given back to us in the Resurrection: Christ is our sanctification (1 Cor 1:30); his Holy Spirit makes this holiness fruitful in external works (2 Thess 2:13); 1 Pet 2:2). Holiness thus means the state of belonging to God and being dedicated to God, in which man, sharing as a member of the Church in the Holy Spirit, has been called to holy service and holy sacrifice—in Christ. Up to this point, then, there is no self-sanctification of man: no sanctification of man by himself, but only by the unmerited grace of God in Jesus Christ through his Holy Spirit.

But there is a "self-sanctification" of man insofar as man himself—not by himself, but he himself—has to sanctify himself. "This is the will of God, your sanctification" (1 Thess 4:3). God's will is the basis and goal of our continued sanctification. This sanctification means behaviour pleasing to God (4:1), which consists in the observance of the commandments (4:2), especially purity of bodily life in refraining from unchasity (4:3), so that even the marriage relationship is fulfilled with sanctification and honour (4:4). "For God has not called us to unchastity, but to sanctification" (4:7). We ought then to dedicate our members to the service of justice for sanctification (Rom 6:19). Thus the fruit of purity is sanctification (Rom 6:22); with modesty we must persevere in it (1 Tim 2:15). We must actively pursue sanctification. Without it, no one will see the Lord (Heb 12:14).

Thus there is such a thing as "self-sanctification," a sanctification in the ethical sense. In the New Testament this is not expressed by the word *hagiazein* (to sanctify). Generally speaking, the meaning of this word is linked to worship, not to ethics. But it is precisely out of the worship character of sanctification that the ethical components arise (cf. the point of contact in Rom 12:1 ff.: the moral life of the Christians as holy sacrifice; cf. Rom 15:16). This judgment of God which justifies has no need of ratification from man. But this sanctifying action of God which segregates man from what is sinful and profane for the service of God peremptorily demands from this chosen man a withdrawal of himself from the world and sin, which is renewed daily. The indicative becomes an imperative, and is its basis: "Let him who is holy sanctify himself still more" (Rev 22:11). In the work of Christ our sanctification is complete and certain, but still it must be continuously fruitful through the power of

Christ's Spirit. Sanctification is a pure gift of God, but it must again and again be laid hold of and carried further by man. The initial giving of oneself in faith to God who justifies and sanctifies must be followed by loving obedience to God's commandments. This is a fulfilment of the law which is at the same time free of the law, through love. Against legalism on the right and libertarianism on the left—the freedom of the children of God.

Ethical sanctification is accomplished through good works, which God in his mercy lets us do (2 Cor 9:8; Eph 2:10; Phil 2:12–16); good works are the fruit of the Spirit (Gal 5:22). We are co-workers with God, *synergoi, cooperatores* (1 Cor 3:9). Man is justified without works, by faith alone. But he is judged according to his works of sanctification (Rom 2:6; 2 Cor 5:10; 2 Tim 4:7 f., 14). In these the genuineness of faith proves itself (Rev 2–3). They are works which are done in God (Jn 3:21), works of faith (1 Thess 1:3; 2 Thess 1:11), which is active in love (Gal 5:6).

The ethical sanctification of man is expressed chiefly by the word *hagiasmos*, "sanctification" (in complete contrast to the use of the word *dikaiōsis*, "justification"). As is clear from the texts cited above, it denotes almost everywhere the moral pattern of life and the moral conduct of man, the practice of holiness and the process of becoming holy. The word *hagiosunē* (holiness: 2 Cor 7:1; 1 Thess 3:13) also, which involves an element of worship rooted in reconciliation, has an ethical character.

But it must always be noticed that there is no autonomous human "self-sanctification". Even where sanctification appears to be man's own doing (1 Pet 1:15–17), it is still rooted in the sanctifying work of redemption of Jesus Christ (1 Pet 2:24). And if Christians ought to keep Christ holy in their hearts (1 Pet 3:15), then it is for the very reason that they are already holy through Christ's grace (1:15 f.; 3:18–22). In this sense the "self-sanctification" of Rev 22:11 can be taken in two ways—in its relation to worship: the holy person should continue to let the sanctification of God act effectively in him; in its relation to ethics: he who is holy should sanctify himself still further. The *hagiazein* (to sanctify) of worship is not to be confused with *hagnizein* (to purify), which carries the idea of ethical "self-sanctification", to render one fit for worship.

The believer, therefore, will never rely on his works, but will always think of himself as a useless servant who has done only what he was obliged to do (Lk 17:9 f.). His own nothingness and his constant dependence on God's grace is only too well known to him. He works out his salvation with fear and trembling, with complete confidence in the workings of God's grace alone (Phil 2:12 f.). He is aware of the temptations which threaten him (1 Cor 7:5; 2 Cor 2:11; Gal. 6:1; 1 Thess 3:5), and the constant possibility of his rejecting God's grace (1 Cor 10:12; 15:58; 16:13). He examines himself (1 Cor 11:28; 2 Cor 13:5; Gal 6:4), and prays to be preserved in faith (1 Thess 3:13; 5:23). And thus he is aware that Jesus Christ has laid hold of him and that he himself does not yet cling irrevocably to him. He knows that he is altogether imperfect and knows what the perfection is toward which he looks forward in expectation.

> It is not as if I had already attained it or had already reached perfection; but I pursue it to see whether I may not lay hold of it, since I have been grasped by Christ Jesus. Dear brethren, I for my part do not consider that I have already made it my own, but one thing I do: I forget what lies behind me, and strain forward towards what lies ahead of me. With the goal placed before my eyes I seek after the prize of victory which God's heavenly call in Christ Jesus sets before me.   [Phil 3:12–14.]

There is no self-justification of man, but there is a "self-sanctification". It is God in Jesus Christ who sanctifies men through his Holy Spirit. But the greatest marvel of God's pure grace is that in the working out of God-given sanctification, man—not by himself, but he himself—may sanctify himself.

6. *From justification to sanctification*
The mere fact that "sanctification" can be expressed by the word *hagiazein* (to sanctify) and *hagiasmos* (sanctification), the first of which suggests religious worship and the second, the ethical dimension, shows that in every discussion of sanctification (and

45

justification) one has to guard against a pernicious ambiguity. To identify God's justification with the ethical sanctification of man is self-reliant Pelagianism. But to separate God's justification from the sanctification (making holy) which takes place in worship and which changes man in his very being, is dead legalism. The justification of God and the sanctification of *man* are to be separated, or better, to be distinguished; to this extent, justification and sanctification are two "steps". God's justification and *God's* sanctification are to be identified; to this extent justification and sanctification are two "sides" of one and the same process. The redemption event in Jesus Christ is a unity, and in him God simultaneously justifies and sacrifices. In justification more is at stake than merely a forgiving declaration of justice; when man is declared just, he is really made just. *Dikaiosunē* (righteousness) is not something which will eventually be given. It is already granted; it is already poured into the present (Rom 3:24–26; 5:1,9,17; 8:30; 9:30; 1 Cor 6:11). It is not just an active property of God, but also a *dōrea*, a gift (Rom 5:17; cf. Rom 9:30; 10:16; Phil 3:9), received by man, which signifies life in the Spirit (Rom 8:10). Even in the earlier polemic epistles, Romans and Galatians, legal justification can never be separated from existence in Christ (Gal 2:16–21; 3:22–29; cf. Rom 5:21) and from union with the Spirit (Gal 3:2–5; 5:5; cf. 1 Cor 6:11). Still, in the controversy with the Judaizers the legal doctrine of justification was necessarily emphasized by Paul in a more

46

isolated way. (The other themes of the doctrine of redemption are not related harmoniously to it, but rather stand alongside of it: thus Rom 3:4: justification by faith alone; Rom 5: reconciliation with God; Rom 6: incorporation into Christ through Baptism; Rom 8; the fruits of the Spirit, etc.) Later on, the more polemic way of treating the subject, which focuses on a single aspect, may be permitted to yield to a more irenic treatment which places it in its over-all context. An example of this might be Phil 3:7–11; it is especially clear in Titus 3:4–7: "But when the goodness of God our Saviour and his love for man appeared, he saved us, not by works of righteousness which we ourselves had performed, but by his own mercy through the bath of rebirth and renewal in the Holy Spirit, which he poured out abundantly upon us through Jesus Christ, our Saviour, so that we, justified through his grace, might become heirs in hope of eternal life."

But though it is certainly true that God's justification is to be identified with *God*'s sanctification, it is no less true that God's justification (and this is the only point which is theologically relevant) is not to be identified with *man's* sanctification. Rather everything depends—precisely in the Pauline way of posing the question—on man's moral sanctification not being justification before God not being its cause. It is just the other way round: God's justification must *lead to* man's ethical sanctification. For St Paul it always held good that the justice attained through the justifying decree (God's *dikaiō-*

47

sis zōēs, "justification which brings life": Rom 5:18), which is linked to the new life (Rom 5:17,21), leads to the sanctification (Rom 6:19) exercised in faithful obedience (Rom 6:16,18), which in its turn again is bound up with all the elements which made up Christ's redemptive action.

Justice does not cling to man in a static way, but, while in man, it is and remains anchored in God's grace. Justice is and remains linked to faith, just as sanctification itself can also be nothing other than an active application and confirmation of the passive receptivity of faith, the constant affirmation proving itself in love, of that which faith receives in justification. Thus the sanctification of man is the fruit of the justification and sanctification of God, perfect if we look to Christ, who is our sanctification (1 Cor 1:30), imperfect if we look at ourselves, who only strive after perfection (Phil 3:12–15; Rom 8:23–25; Gal 5:5), subject to temptation, exposed to struggle, a life of death to self to live for God in Christ. "Let the just man continue to go forward in righteousness, and him who is holy sanctify himself yet more! Behold, I am coming soon . . ." (Rev 22:11 f.).

2. Liturgical Reform and Christian Unity

"It is the goal of this most sacred Council to intensify the daily growth of Catholics in Christian living; to make more responsive to the requirements of our times those Church observances which are open to adaptation; to nurture whatever can contribute to the unity of all who believe in Christ; and to strengthen those aspects of the Church which can help summon all of mankind into its embrace."—*Constitution on the Sacred Liturgy*, Introduction, 1.

Present-day Reform of the Mass

The renewal of worship and the Liturgy is a task of great moment in the history of the Church. What the Second Vatican Council decided in this respect will be no less important for the Church and for Christianity as a whole than the decisions regarding liturgical reform which faced the Council of Trent after the decline of the late Middle Ages. It is precisely for this reason that it is extremely important for us to examine the historical background, since it is only when they are viewed in this perspective that the decisions of Vatican II can be properly understood and evaluated. All the same, the opinion has been voiced. in many dioceses and parishes, that the Council's liturgical renewal is in fact no more than a series of innovations which are in direct contradiction to the good old Catholic tradition. There are, alas, far too many people who, because of a basic lack of knowledge, see the "old tradition" as one and the same thing as what happened in their younger days, although, in comparison with the 2,000-year-old history of the Church and her liturgy, those younger days are young indeed!

Theologians Today: Hans Küng

It is necessary here to point out straightaway that the renewal of the Liturgy which is in process is fully supported by the very best of the old Catholic tradition, that what seems to be new today is basically of the greatest antiquity, and that what may have to go is in fact not part of the old tradition but of relatively recent innovations. We are not going into this simply because it is of historical interest: Our examination of the historical background is based far more on pastoral considerations, since what the Council had in mind was the renewal of the Church as a preparation for the reunion of all separated Christians, with ecclesiastical worship as the central point of this renewal. And this renewal of Christian worship in conformity to the prevalent conditions of a new age can only be good if it is derived from the Gospel of Christ, from its origins. In the Catholic Mass, what ultimately matters is simply that the Lord's command, "Do this in memory of me", is obediently carried out. Do *this*, and not this, that or the other, however beautiful, impressive or long-established it may be. But is it not true to say that this very thing that our Lord commanded us to do has become obscured over the centuries? Has it not in fact been said, half jokingly, half seriously, that if the Apostle Paul himself happened to go into the average Catholic church while High Mass was being celebrated, he would have great difficulty in understanding, unless somebody explained it to him, that what was taking place here was the fulfilment of the Lord's command to "do this in memory of me"?

Liturgical Reform and Christian Unity

What the present reform of the liturgy aims to do is once again to make the original structure of Christian worship, which derives from the Gospel, more clear and understandable for the people. The pattern of the liturgy of the ancient Church cannot, of course, be slavishly copied. What the ancient liturgy can provide, however, is a model which brings the organic structure of Christian worship well to the fore and which can, in this sense, also be adapted to modern needs.

In such a short exposition it is impossible to make a complete survey of the entire history even of the Roman Mass, let alone of the many other rites. All that I can do here is to make the reader aware of a few salient points so that he will recognize what is essential in this historical development and understand the background facts of the Council's Constitution on the Liturgy. To this end, I shall briefly review four typical images of the Mass throughout the centuries. None of the examples which follow is a poetic fabrication. They have been chosen because they conform closely to the most recent research into the history of the Liturgy.

First Example: Mass celebrated in a house in the second century. Let us imagine that we are back in the earliest Christian times in Rome, during the oppression and persecution of the Church. Christians form an insignificant minority. We are looking into a room. It is a dining-hall. The Eucharist would have been celebrated, a short time ago, in this room, the

53

celebration taking place, just as it did during the Last Supper, while the meal was in progress. Now, however, the dining-room has become an assembly hall. All the tables have disappeared except one. The leader of the assembly, a bishop or priest, who is dressed in the clothes of a Roman citizen, is standing at this table. He is facing the people.

Perfectly ordinary bread and wine have been brought along. The bishop now begins, in Greek, not in Latin, the prayer of thanksgiving, the *eucharistia*. The biblical words of consecration are inserted into this single prayer of thanksgiving. At the end of the prayer all those who are present say "Amen" and receive—standing—the gifts, which are now no longer bread and wine, but the body and blood of Jesus Christ. This is the Mass as it has been handed down to us by Justin the Martyr (*c.* A.D. 150)—an extremely simple celebration, consisting of a single "prayer of thanksgiving" and the meal or communion of all those present, and for this reason called the "Eucharistia". The oldest Roman eucharistic formula that has been preserved comes from Hippolytus of Rome (*c.* A.D. 215). This gives us a very fine idea of what the ancient Mass looked like. The gifts are placed on the table and the Mass, or prayer of thanksgiving, begins. Together with the priests who are present, the bishop extends his hands over the gifts and begins: "The Lord be with you." The people reply: "And with thy spirit." "Lift up your hearts!" "We have lifted them up to the Lord." "Let us give thanks to the Lord!" "It is meet and just." Then the bishop continues: "We give thee thanks, O God, through thy beloved servant (*pais, puer*) Jesus Christ, whom thou hast sent to us in recent times as our saviour and redeemer and the herald of thy new dispensation. He is thy undivided Word, thou hast made everything through him, and it was well pleasing to thee. Thou didst send him from heaven into the womb of the Virgin and, carried in the womb, he became flesh and was revealed as thy Son, born by the Holy Spirit of the Virgin. In that he fulfilled thy will and won for thee a holy people, he extended his hands in suffering, to redeem from suffering those who believe in him. And since he was handed over, a willing victim, to suffering, to deprive death of its power and to break the chains binding us to the devil and to trample hell underfoot and to enlighten the just and to mark an epoch and to proclaim the Resurrection, he took the bread and, giving thanks to thee, said: Take and eat, this is my body, that is broken for you. Likewise he took the chalice. saying: This is my blood, that is shed for you. Whenever you do this, do it in my memory. Mindful also of his death and resurrection, we offer the bread and the chalice, giving thanks to thee for deeming us worthy to stand before thee and serve thee. And we ask thee to send the Holy Ghost down upon this offering of thy holy Church. Bringing her together in unity, do thou bestow on all thy saints who receive it the fullness of the Holy Spirit, to confirm our faith in truth, so that we may praise and glorify thee through thy servant Jesus Christ, through whom is

55

praise and honour to the Father, to the Son and to the Holy Ghost, in thy holy Church, now and for ever and ever. Amen." Communion followed immediately after this, the faithful receiving the offerings, taking the bread in their open hands. At quite an early date, although it did not always take place, a Service of the Word was held in association with the celebration of the Eucharist, in imitation of the synagogue service. A series of texts from the Old and New Testaments were read, without a break, and explained, there were communal prayers and psalms were sung. What can we learn from this ancient form of the Mass?

(1) The basic structure of the Mass is quite simple and easy to understand. It consists essentially of the prayer of thanksgiving, which incorporates the commemorative words of consecration, and the eucharistic meal. This basic structure was preserved throughout the centuries, despite frequent later additions and accretions. In its essence it does not depart from the Last Supper, and we know it from scriptural sources.

(2) In its early form the Mass was quite flexible. Only the essential outlines of the celebration were fixed. Each bishop or priest used his own discretion in shaping the Liturgy. The language was the vernacular of the period; thus, the language used in the celebration of the oldest form of the Roman liturgy known to us was not, as many believe, Latin but *koinē* Greek, the current vernacular of the Roman Empire. The entire service was an intimate commu-

nal feast, during which the people prayed and sang together.

(3) All those who were present at the meal also received the sacrament in both kinds, bread *and* wine. It would have struck these early Christians as completely absurd to be present at a meal without eating, or to receive the sacrament either before Mass or before the eucharistic prayer was over. It would have seemed preposterous to them if several masses were celebrated simultaneously in the same place. If more than one priest were present, then concelebration took place, all the priests saying a single Mass together with the chief celebrant.

Second Example: Mass celebrated in a basilica in the fifth and the sixth centuries. Christianity has by now spread throughout the entire Roman Empire. Let us imagine ourselves to be present in one of these splendid Roman basilicas of the period. Here, too, the wooden table, or altar, is placed well to the fore and the priest celebrates the same Mass, once again facing the people and once again dressed in the clothes of a Roman citizen. But there have been many changes during the intervening centuries.

Everything has become longer, grander and more solemn. Various intercessions, for the living, the dead, special petitions for the Church and so on, have been inserted into the simple, ancient eucharistic prayer of thanksgiving. These intercessions are linked with the names of martyrs, to whom more and more honour is now—since the time of Christian persecution—being paid. Furthermore there are, in addition to the prayer of thanksgiving, three important new elements: the singing of a psalm, accompanied by a prayer, on the entry of the clergy into the basilica (the introductory psalm or Introit), a second psalm while the faithful bring their offerings of bread, wine and other gifts (the Offertory), and a third psalm during the communion of the faithful (the Communion chant). At the same time, the Mass has above all been, as we would say now, *solemnized*. A whole set of ceremonies have been borrowed from the Byzantine–Roman court ceremonial, including many which the earliest Christians had rejected as heathen practices—genuflections, bowing, kissing, such things as incense, candles and so on, and such marks of distinction as the stole or the ring. As a result of this solemnization of the Mass, a more artistic form of chant was gradually replacing the earlier, simpler singing of the people. What, then, can we learn from this example?

(1) It goes without saying that the Liturgy of this period had adapted itself to the change which had taken place in the vernacular. Since the people of Rome no longer used Greek, but Latin, the liturgical language had changed from Greek to Latin.

(2) A whole host of involved ceremonies, which take place particularly in solemn High Mass and which today have a disturbing effect upon people who prefer to aim at simplicity and straightforwardness, in that these ceremonies distract from what is essential, can be traced directly to the Byzantine–

58

Roman court ceremonial, and thus cannot be regarded as part of the unchangeable essence of the Mass.

(3) The adaptation of the Mass to the celebration of special feasts in honour of the saints is closely connected with the then prevalent cult of the martyrs and is thus a later development.

Third Example: Mass during the High Middle Ages. The centre of world civilization had by this time moved northwards away from Rome and political leadership had, in the eighth and ninth centuries, passed into the hands of the Frankish emperors. A parallel movement took place at about the same time in the case of the Liturgy, which had hitherto been confined to Rome and its environs (and its sphere of influence, as, for example, the mission to the Anglo-Saxons). Not only the ordinary parochial liturgy, but also the solemn papal liturgy, were transferred to the Frankish Empire, with many serious consequences.

Until this time, there had been no such thing as silent, low Mass. All the prayers of the Mass, including the words of consecration, had, for obvious reasons, been spoken aloud, as they were by Christ. Now, however, many silent, or quietly uttered, prayers were added to the Mass, once again close to the beginning (the Gradual), during the preparation of the offerings and at the Communion. We find the priest saying prayers continuously at the altar, even during the actions of the Mass. At this time, too, we find the practice of silent, or quietly spoken, priestly

59

prayer gradually spreading even to the oldest prayers of the Mass, including the ancient prayer of thanksgiving (the Canon) and the words of consecration incorporated into it. One obvious reason for this is that the people no longer understood Latin.

One consequence of this was, of course, a gradual estrangement between the people and the altar. This arose because the language of the Liturgy was no longer understood by the people, because the various solemn, ceremonial actions, such as genuflection, signs of the cross and the use of incense, were rapidly increasing in number and in importance, and, finally, because the choir, where the clergy assembled, was separated from the nave of the church, where the people were. A "high altar", placed right up against the apse, replaced the older altar which used to stand close to the people. Again, we find the priest now no longer celebrating Mass facing the people, but facing the wall, and, what is more, no longer able to see over the superstructure of the altar, because it has become so high. As the Mass is no longer visible and understandable, it has to be interpreted in a new and allegorical way for the sake of the people, and they begin to see it as a dramatic representation of the life of Jesus—as a play or spectacle. The original meaning of the Mass as a celebration in thanksgiving and in commemoration of the Last Supper is often lost. The people do nothing. They simply see the action of the Mass, and that is why the traditional garments, or vestments, which had been preserved since the time of

Rome's supremacy, gave way at this period to similar vestments which changed in colour according to a definite plan. It is for the same reason that, despite violent opposition on the part of the ecclesiastical authorities, the practice of the priest's elevation of the sacred body and blood and his adoration by genuflection was introduced for the first time in the thirteenth century. The reception of the Sacrament in Communion became the exception rather than the normal rule, but the people wanted at least to be able to see the sacred species. At the same time, ordinary bread disappeared from the altar and was gradually replaced by the "host", which was un-leavened and snow-white and, in appearance, quite unlike ordinary bread. Moreover, whereas in the ancient Church, all the priests who were present celebrated one and the same Mass together, we find each priest now saying his own Mass separately, and, to permit this practice, more and more side-altars being built adjacent to the original single altar. Finally, what can we learn from this third example?

(1) This period saw the emergence of a deep gulf between the priest and the people. This is very far from the original mind of the Church, but the gulf has persisted throughout the centuries and can often only be overcome nowadays after a long and some-times painful struggle.

(2) During this period, too, Communion became a separate rite, and was administered, moreover, more and more frequently, in one kind only. Earlier in the history of the Church, Communion during

Mass was the norm; during this period of the Middle Ages, however, it was exceptional. Before this time, the Bread of Life was, as Jesus commanded, eaten. Since then, it has more often been beheld and adored. The recent introduction of the monstrance bears witness to this.

(3) Whereas there was previously only one altar in any given church and only one Mass celebrated at any given time, from this time onwards many masses could be celebrated simultaneously at many different altars in the same church. The "private" Mass had come into being.

Fourth Example: Mass since the Tridentine reform of 1570. This is, to all intents and purposes, the Mass which we had until recently. In the first place, the reforms made by the Council of Trent cut out the rank and monstrous excesses which had, particularly during the later Middle Ages, crept into the Mass. In the second place, the council's reforms had regularized the Mass down to the last detail, thus doing something which had never been attempted before. For this reason, the post-tridentine Mass is often called the "Mass of the rubrics". As literally everything had been regulated down to the last word and the tiniest detail of the position of the celebrant's fingers, and, what is more, since the people were still given no opportunity of taking an active part in the celebration, their private and personal piety began to express itself with great energy and accompanying emotion in an ever-increasing number of different devotions. What happened all too frequently was that the Mass was regarded as just one among many devotions, although it probably remained the most important. More candles were lit during these various devotions than at Mass itself. Meanwhile, in Europe, what has been called the "exodus" had come about. Sunday Mass was no longer fully attended. In many different European countries, the fact that only a small number of the faithful regularly went to Sunday Mass was recognized with horror. This, of course, had the most far-reaching effects on the religious life of the people as a whole. It is not true to say that it is exclusively the form of the Mass which is at fault here, though it is certainly one of the causes which can be blamed. It is thus not difficult to understand why many countermeasures have been introduced since that time by the Church leaders, beginning with Pius x, who urged frequent Communion and the active participation of the people in Christian worship, right down to Pius xii and the most recent reforms. It is basically a question of overcoming the 1,000-year-old gulf between the people and the priest at the altar, and of once again making clear to the people the original structure of the Eucharist.

Liturgical Reform and Christian Unity

Has liturgical reform really any *ecumenical* significance? One might almost go so far as to say that the fact that a *beginning* has already been made with the reform of the Liturgy is in itself of ecumenical importance. Going contrary to certain trends which pointed in other directions, or were less in line with ecumenical considerations, the Council decided to deal with the liturgy first. From the ecumenical point of view, this decision had two important consequences:

(1) *A concentration on the practical needs of pastoral care.* In this way the Council avoided the danger of becoming too preoccupied with doctrine to the exclusion of everything else. The danger which constantly threatens the World Council of Churches, which is unable to assume any unity either in the message or in the teaching of its individual members —or at most only a minimum of unity—is that of becoming preoccupied with pragmatic considerations, with the result that practical work is overemphasized and too little value is placed on the importance of doctrine. On the other hand, the danger facing a Council of the Catholic Church, which can in fact assume unity in its message and teaching, is that doctrine is overstressed and practical work receives too little attention, since the Church always tends to be immersed in doctrinal problems. Catholic theologians especially—this fortunately applies to a far lesser extent in the case of the bishops—are always inclined to overestimate the need for constant elucidation of the Church's teaching. Would it be of any value at all today to the Church or to the world, simply to restate old doctrines? "There is no need to summon a Council to do this", John XXIII

himself, said in his inaugural address. Would it, moreover, benefit either the Church or the world to pass judgment upon all those whose teaching is in error? The Church "prefers to use the medicine of mercy rather than severity, and it believes that it can demonstrate the value of its teaching by aligning itself more closely to the needs of today rather than by using the weapon of judgment and condemnation", the Pope said, with certain innate tendencies on the part of the Church to overemphasize doctrinal questions clearly in mind. The settlement of doctrinal differences between individual Catholic schools of theological thought never has been, and is not now, the task of a council. It would also not be opportune to try to settle differences in doctrine between the individual Christian denominations—these will have to be gone over slowly and thoroughly by the theologians, from the exegetical, historical and dogmatic points of view. The Council cannot replace the work of the theologians, and, in any case, a premature attempt to resolve highly controversial issues of doctrine would do the gravest disservice to the ecumenical cause.

Liturgical reform and a concentration of effort upon the practical aspects of pastoral care —these are the important, positive features in all attempts towards reunion. The *Constitution on the Liturgy* does not lay down anything dogmatically. Thus it is evident that it is quite possible for the Church to be renewed, and for a positive forward thrust to be given to the movement towards a closer under-

c

standing between the various Christian communions, without previously clearing up every theoretical question. Undoubtedly the most promising approach to ecumenical approximation today is to smooth the way, but a practical renewal, based on the Gospel rather than on one particular theology, for later theological discussions.

(2) *A concentration on central problems.* The Council avoided the danger of allowing itself to be sidetracked from the central problems. The First Vatican Council dealt with many questions of ecclesiastical discipline which were peripheral, and consequently not the concern of an ecumenical council. There was similarly many questions for discussion by the Second Vatican Council which were certainly important—for example, the problems raised by the films, television and the Press, problems of ecclesiastical trusteeship and allied questions —but which in comparison with the intrinsic task of the Church, were no more than fringe problems. It is Christian worship which is, and must always be, central in the life of the Church. If success is achieved in renewing the Church's liturgy, the effects of this renewal will be felt in every sphere of activity within the Church. If Catholic worship is successfully re-fashioned in a more ecumenical form, the effect on the whole movement towards reunion with the separated Christians will be decisive. The Protestant Reformers, too, regarded liturgical renewal as a task of central importance, and it was one of their most insistent demands. The Council of Trent carried out

considerable reforms in the sphere of Catholic worship by removing many appalling abuses and by rearranging the form of the Catholic liturgy. But the Tridentine reforms were in fact more in the nature of a restoration of the medieval *status quo* than a truly constructive and creative renewal of Christian worship in the light of the Gospel and arising from a need to adapt worship to the requirements of a new age. It must be remembered, however, that the Council of Trent did not have all the findings of modern historical and liturgical research at its disposal. No positive answer could be given to many of the demands made by the Reformers at the time of the Council of Trent, and that even now these questions are still unresolved. From this point of view as well, then, it is of the utmost importance in the cause of the reunion of separated Christianity to give precedence to liturgical reform and to concentrate on the central problems of renewal.

Should Protestant claims be taken into consideration in Liturgical Reform?

(1) *A closer approximation to the pattern of the Last Supper*. One of the main objections on the part of the Reformers was that the Mass had developed into a pure "ceremony" which had basically little more to do with the Last Supper. Indeed, they claimed that it had become so overgrown with rank abuses and misinterpretation that it had become idolatry.

We Catholics, on the other hand, maintained that

the essential element of the Mass—"Do this in memory of me"—has always been preserved, though it cannot be denied that the original and inherent fundamental structure of the eucharistic element in the Mass has become overlaid and obscured by inessentials over the centuries. In its original form the Mass was a simple and universally intelligible celebration, consisting of thanksgiving and the sacred meal. The essential elements of the Mass were the *eucharistia*—a single prayer of thanksgiving, often freely improvised, in the course of which the words of consecration were repeated—and the partaking of the consecrated gifts. The language of the Mass was the language of the people and the signs were quite clear—ordinary bread and ordinary wine were used, and everyone present received both the body *and* the blood of the Lord. This original basic structure of the Mass became partially obscured with the passage of time—by the insertion of new elements into the eucharistic prayer of thanksgiving and by numerous extraneous additions, by the continued use of an incomprehensible liturgical language and by the practice of praying the most important parts of the Mass silently, by the unnecessary multiplicity of external details, by an increasing "solemnization" in the form of public worship which was often extremely ill-adapted to pastoral needs, by the gradual neglect of the commemorative aspect of the Mass, and so on.

The aim of the *Constitution on the Liturgy* has been to make the Church's celebration of the

Eucharist conform more clearly and more closely to the Last Supper which Jesus celebrated with his apostles, by reforming the entire rite, by bringing what is essential well to the fore, by suppressing what is inessential, by shortening the rite, by eliminating all unnecessary repetitions, by accepting once again all that is good in the ancient tradition of the Church and so on. A very important feature is the restoration of the ancient eucharistic prayer and, in conjunction with this, the reform of the Canon of the Mass. This successful attempt to make the celebration of the Eucharist approximate more closely to the Last Supper must be of the greatest ecumenical importance.

(2) *The hearing of the word of God.* Another of the reproaches which the reformers levelled against the Catholic Church was that the word of God was no longer heard in Catholic worship. The message, they held, was proclaimed in an unintelligible language, the biblical texts were not elucidated and preaching was seriously neglected.

From the earliest period in the history of the Catholic Church, the reading of Holy Scripture has an honourable place, and at a very early stage a Service of the Word, consisting of readings, prayers and singing, was held in conjunction with the eucharistic celebration. At that time, the entire Scripture was read aloud and commented upon in public services. St Augustine, for example, spent weeks and months expounding the Psalms, Genesis, the Gospels and so on, verse by verse to his com-

69

munity. In the Middle Ages too, the word of God was proclaimed by the Church, though it cannot be denied that, by this time, the preaching of the Word was in a pretty bad way. The people no longer understood the language, comparatively short extracts were read from the whole of the Old and New Testaments, and the essential task of the Church to proclaim the word of God was frequently not treated very seriously. The contemporary movement for liturgical renewal has aimed at giving the preaching of the Word a new importance within the framework of public worship, by introducing the intelligible reading of Holy Scripture in the vernacular, by arranging a new cycle of passages from Scripture, covering several years rather than, as before, only one, and thus providing for the reading of those texts which have hitherto been neglected, by giving greater emphasis to the sermon, and by allowing the spirit of Holy Scripture to penetrate the whole of the Liturgy, including the hymns and various devotions. Non-Catholic Christians will surely agree wholeheartedly that, if these new measures for the word of God to be heard and taken more seriously in Catholic worship are fully carried out, the effect on the whole work of renewing the Church and its preparation for reunion with separated Christians will be decisive.

(3) *Worship by the entire priestly people.* A further criticism made by the Reformers was that the liturgy of the Middle Ages had become, like the medieval Church itself, sacerdotalized. The people were, to a

very great extent, excluded, and only the priest played an active part in religious worship.

In the early Church, the people contributed a very active part to the Liturgy—there were communal prayers and singing, the body of the Lord was eaten and the blood of the Lord was drunk, together. When the regional liturgy of Rome was imposed on the Frankish Empire, the consequence was without doubt, a strict exclusion of the people. They did not understand the Latin language. Their share in the Liturgy was restricted to watching passively. The Mass, divorced, as far as they were concerned, from its words, was given an allegorical and quite arbitrary interpretation. The essential features of the Mass became more and more obscured by the ever-increasing solemnization of the ceremonial. The altar table, which had originally been situated close to the people, was elaborated into a "high" altar and placed away from them in the apse, where Mass was celebrated facing the wall, instead of facing the people, as before. The clergy, in the choir, were separated from the people in the nave by the rood-screen. The practice of general Communion among the people ceased because of an exaggerated reverence for the Sacrament, and an unnecessary insistence on the moral conditions, fasting regulations and so on.

It was the aim of the movement for liturgical renewal so to remodel religious worship that it might once again become the worship of the entire priestly people. For decades, the chief aim of those

who were working for a renewal of the Liturgy had
been to secure for the people an active share in the
whole Liturgy. Much of this has now been inauga-
rated by Vatican II: the Liturgy has become fully
intelligible, communal prayer and singing and a
communal partaking of the eucharistic feast have
been reintroduced, as also has Communion in both
kinds, the vernacular has replaced parts, and so on.
All this provides a positive answer to the genuine
demands of Protestant Christians.

(4) *Adaptation to the needs of the various peoples
within the Church.* Another of the Reformers'
criticisms was that the Church, and consequently
its public worship, had become excessively "Roman-
ized". Its liturgy was insufficiently suited to the
needs of the different peoples and races within the
Church. This criticism was applied to the whole
spirit of the Liturgy, as well as to its structure,
language, music, gestures and movements.

In the early Christian period, almost every local
Church worked out its own individual liturgical
pattern, with the result that an impressive number
of Eastern and Western rites came into being within
the one Church. The same, yet a different, Mass was
celebrated according to the Greek, Roman, Ethio-
pian, Armenian, Syriac, Mozarabic, Slavonic or
other rites. It was towards the end of the sixth
century that the liturgy of Rome was passed on, by
the Roman monks, to the Anglo-Saxon mission, In
the Frankish Empire, however, it was the Frankish
princes and prelates themselves who suppressed

the older, native Gallican liturgy and introduced the liturgy which had previously been in use only in Rome and her immediate environs. The motives behind this were clearly cultural and political rather than pastoral. Although the Roman liturgy underwent many changes when it was transferred from Rome to the Frankish Empire—one of the most notable being the energemce of the Gregorian chant, which we sing nowadays, not according to the early Roman tradition, but in the form in which it has been handed down to us by the Franks—the fact remains that the Liturgy as a whole was in many respects a foreign one to the peoples north of the Alps. The foreign language itself was sufficient to prevent the Roman rite from becoming a genuine people's liturgy among the Germanic tribes. The same problem arose at a more recent date, in an even more acute form, when the local liturgy of Rome was transferred from Europe to other continents with totally different cultures.

The present-day aims in liturgical renewal include the complete readaptations of public worship to the needs of every individual racial group, so that the liturgy of the Church may once more become a genuine liturgy of the people. What the movement for liturgical renewal stands for could be summed up in the phrase "unity, but not uniformity". It should be perfectly possible to adapt the Liturgy to suit the needs of each race or people by adapting the language, gestures and movements of the Liturgy, the form and content of the prayers, the singing and the arrangement of the music and the entire structure of the rite. It is also quite possible to envisage the introduction of new rites in the missionary territories. The conscious development of genuine people's liturgies certainly meets the legitimate claims of Protestant Christianity.

Catholic and Protestant Collaboration

It is to be hoped that Christians outside the Catholic Church will not simply take note of the efforts which the Catholic Church has made and is making to advance the cause of Christian reunion, and remain content to refer rather complacently to the reformation which has already take place in their worship. A reaction of this kind would, in the Catholic view, imply a onesided attitude on the part of Protestant Christians. It is rather to be hoped that those Christians outside the Catholic Church will make every effort to examine their own position very carefully and to approach the Catholic Church more closely from their side, too, in a constructive and ecumenical spirit. The central point of controversy alone—that of the priestly office and function and its significance in the sphere of public worship—provides sufficient basis for serious ecumenical thought. It should be possible to prepare the way for the reunion of separated Christianity along these lines, in a constructive and positive manner, so long as this is done by both Catholic and Protestant Christians.

3. Freedom in the World

"Authentic freedom is an exceptional sign of the divine image within man. For God has willed that man be left 'in the hand of his own counsel' so that he can seek his Creator spontaneously, and come freely to utter and blissful perfection through loyalty to him. Such a choice is personally motivated and prompted from within. . . . Before the judgment seat of God each man must render an account of his own life, whether he has done good or evil."—*Pastoral Constitution on the Church in the Modern World*, I, 1, 17.

A Saint in the World?

Looking at the famous painting of Thomas More by Hans Holbein, we often ask ourselves: Is this the face of a "saint"? It is indeed a wonderful face: the eyes are serenely thoughtful, critical, you might almost say sceptical, yet not hard, but kindly; the nose and mouth indicate discipline and moderation, unforced assurance and firmness; the whole is of a simple, natural cast, making it a likeable face. A fine, strong face; but a saint's face?

We can almost read the man's past history from the face: student at Oxford at fourteen, and afterwards in London; at twenty-two, the friend of Erasmus of Rotterdam and himself a brilliant humanist and jurist; at twenty-six, Member of Parliament; then Under-Sheriff of the City of London and Reader in Law at Lincon's Inn; diplomat and ambassador at thirty-seven; Under-Treasurer of England at forty-three; then Speaker of the Lower House, and High Steward of the Universities of Oxford and Cambridge; finally, at fifty-one, Lord Chancellor and first statesman of the realm. Such was Sir Thomas More, whose picture ("immeasurably more beautiful than any reproduction of it") Holbein has given us. But once again: Is this the picture of a saint?

This is not an idle question for the Christian who is trying to live by the Gospel in the world. Because it is not posed abstractly and theoretically, but attached to a concrete, existing human being, it can be made an extremely pressing test question on one's own Christian existence in the world. Only too often the Christian comes up against the question whether it is possible at all to live as a Christian in the world; meaning, not just to get along somehow, but to live by the Gospel. Rather, if one really wants to live by the Gospel, does one not have to forsake the world and retire into the desert or into a monastery? Thomas More lived in the world; indeed, he was what is called "a man of the world". Urbane, self-assured, distinguished, with perfect manners (learnt in boyhood in the household of Lord Chancellor Morton), this great scholar, diplomat and orator had a command not only of Latin but also—a matter of hard labour to the early humanists—of Greek, and was at the same time a supreme master of English prose. He was personally acquainted with the greatest scholars not only of England (Colet, Grocyn, Linacre) but of all Europe, and conducted an extensive correspondence: with the Spaniard Vives, the Frenchman Budé, the Dutchman Erasmus; Holbein was for a long while his guest. His history of Richard III, which had a profound influence on Shakespeare, was the start of English historical writing. His *Utopia*, the first of a whole series of "ideal states", is, with Machiavelli's *Prince*, which appeared in the same year, the most influential book on the State produced in the sixteenth century. Yet this man of the world with his towering intelligence, his iron resolution, his high sense of justice and his fearless bearing (of which he had given evidence as a young man in Parliament, when, regardless of danger, he spoke in a financial debate against the miserly Henry VII), was at the same time possessed of an enchanting modesty, friendliness and amiability. *Gravitas* with both *suavitas* and *festivitas* were his characteristics, according to the witness of contemporaries. Deep seriousness was coupled in this "man for all seasons" with a humour that became proverbial. Even in his boyhood as a page he had been an excellent actor (and wrote little plays himself); he was one of the greatest masters of irony, so that Erasmus, punning on his name, dedicated to him that one of his works which is most popular in character, the *Moriae Encomium*, or *Praise of Folly*. More had the trick of producing his jests with so solemn a countenance that even his own family was constantly taken in by them; jest and earnest were never easy to distinguish in him.

Is it any wonder that Sir Thomas More was admired throughout Europe and that there were those in England who consciously imitated him? There was a man "who, being most unlike unto him in wit and learning, nevertheless in wearing his gown awry upon the one shoulder, as Sir Thomas

79

More was wont to do, would needs be counted like unto him". "Thomas More, Lord Chancellor of England, whose soul was more pure than any snow, whose genius was such as England never had—yea, and never shall have again, mother of good wits though England be . . ." So wrote Erasmus on receiving the news of More's death. Thomas More; great genius, great humanist. Thomas More—a great "saint" as well? The Gospel demands more than pure, noble *humanitas;* the following of Christ more than creative genius.

Property, Family, State

When we look at this man, does it seem as though the Sermon on the Mount had counted for anything with him? This is the question which we here focus on Thomas More, but whose application is to us, who are Christians in the world. It can be made more explicit by reference to the envangelical "counsels" (often misunderstood in the sense of a two-level morality) of poverty, celibacy and obedience. It is true that this listing together of the three evangelical counsels represents a later theological systematization. But the first two have their basis directly in the New Testament. And even though it is not possible in principle to measure all Christian existence by them and them alone, yet when properly, i.e., scripturally, understood they can face the Christian in the world with an acutely critical question.

There is no escaping the impression that Thomas More was committed in exactly the opposite direction. Christian sociologists often give the three pillars of the social order as the family, property, and the State. They explain them like this: The task that God has given man is the individual working out of the fulfilment of his own person within his human nature. First, the fulfilment of the human person as it were inwards; the community of marriage, through mutual, loving self-giving and the support and upbringing of the children. Hence the social institution and function of the *family*, because this is the only way of guaranteeing a sensible ordering of things in this sphere. At the same time, the human person must be fulfilled in an outward direction; by addressing himself to the world of material things without which man's life is impossible. Hence the social institution and function of *private property*, as the one way in which material goods can give the free human personality its full development and value, the one way of taking care of the future for the individual and his family, and finally the one way of preserving and advancing the common good, social order and social peace. But because family relationships and economic relationships are, independently of each other, in a constant state of change, and because these two spheres of life exist in relation to each other in a state of dialectical tension and development, there has to be regulation by law, and there has to be a power which gives that law permanence. Hence the social institution and function of the *State*, which—not as the only guarantee of the rule of law, yet as its

81

highest guarantee—has the task of co-ordinating the rights and duties of individuals and providing them with a permanent structure, so that the human person may thus pursue its full and lasting integration in security and peace.

Thus speak the sociologists. The family, private property, and the State as guaranteeing the rule of law, are according to them necessary to the fulfilment of man's task in life, to man's realization of himself as a person. Precisely in this way—because man can only exist as a social being—they are necessary for the ordering of the whole life of the community, at the family, social and political levels. Family, property and State appear as the three pillars of order in the life of society.

But is it not strange to see how, to the scandal of sociologists, these very pillars of order are, for the Christian setting out to follow Christ, called in question by the Gospel? If we look at the three props and stays of order and the three evangelical "counsels", is it not striking how precisely they correspond to each other, or rather contradict each other? Christian perfection is to consist in poverty, celibacy and obedience. Does not freely chosen poverty contradict property, freely chosen celibacy, the family, and freely chosen obedience, as a renunciation of rights and power, that binding rule of law which the State is there to guarantee?

But Thomas More seems to have stood very firmly indeed by these three principal pillars of the secular social order.

Property: Sir Thomas had an extremely fine house in London, on the banks of the Thames at Chelsea, with a library, a gallery, a chapel, a park and orchard. He maintained a numerous household, and his house was full of curious and remarkable things; anything that came from abroad or was otherwise of great interest he would buy immediately, and it gave him pleasure when other people took delight in these things. He took particular pleasure in studying the forms and characteristics of animals. He kept a whole menagerie, with innumerable species of birds and other rare animals: beavers, weasels, foxes. . . . His great favourite was his monkey, immortalized as part of the More family portrait and praised for its cleverness by Erasmus, who had watched it engaged in a game with a weasel. Thus Thomas More, who took particular pleasure in fools and himself maintained a fool as part of his household, lived a happy life in the midst of his family and his numerous friends and visitors, "with no aversion from innocent pleasure".

Family: At the age of twenty-seven or twenty-eight Sir Thomas married the seventeen-year-old Jane Colt, whom he dearly loved and tried to educate. She bore him three daughters, Margaret, Cecily and Elisabeth, and one son, John. After the early death of his wife he married a second time; Dame Alice, elderly and not very amiable, was at least a good housewife. He was greatly attached to his children. He gave his daughters the same humanist education as his son, well aware of this as a bold innovation

83

which would bring him criticism. Margaret, in particular, attained a noteworthy degree of learning, with much-admired latinity. More thought of his children throughout all the demands made on him by his activity as a statesman, even when on embassies or journeying in attendance on the King. He expected a letter from each of them every day. He answered them in Latin prose or Latin verses, and wrote these even when riding, soaked through with rain, on a horse stumbling or stuck in the mud. He loves to remember how he has given them fine silk clothes and fed them with cakes and fruit, and beaten them, when strictly necessary, only with peacocks' feathers. Is it any wonder that More's foster-daughter, Margaret Gigs, used to commit small faults simply for the pleasure of being scolded and noticed by More?

The State: Sir Thomas More's whole life was devoted to the State and the defence of the rule of law. In his native city of London, his name became a legend above all for his work as a judge. Never before or after in England had every man come by his own so well and so swiftly. "Howbeit, this one thing, son", said More to one of his sons-in-law, "I assure thee on my faith, that if the parties will at my hands call for justice, then, all were it my father stood on the one side, and the Devil on the other, his cause being good, the Devil should have right." There are many anecdotes illustrating More's display of the wisdom of Solomon. Under More's predecessor as Chancellor, Wolsey, business had piled up enormously. When More took office, there were cases outstanding that had been introduced twenty years before. His profound knowledge of the law and his astonishing gift of quick comprehension brought him to that day of triumph when he took his seat, settled a case, called for the next one—and there were no more to come. He had the fact recorded in the public acts of the Court. Along with his humour, it was this above all that made him a legend. Decades later, the epigrams were praising him:

> When More some time had Chancellor been,
>   No more suits did remain.
> The like will never more be seen
>   Till More be there again.

More carried out all his State business with the same combination of deliberation and devotion. Unlike Erasmus, who was at home nowhere and everywhere, he was filled with a genuinely English, and at the same time European, patriotism, which even led him into a quarrel with a French humanist on behalf of his native land. More the politician, who had already shown in *Utopia* his interest in translantic discoveries and colonization, devoted himself entirely, in a manner totally different from his predecessor Wolsey, to maintaining England and the Continent of Europe in peace. It was thus that he sought, in all loyalty, to serve his king, whose ambitions were bent upon the Continent. How thoroughly More was involved with secular power is most vividly shown to

85

us in that picture transmitted by his son-in-law Roper: Henry VIII, an unexpected guest to dinner at Chelsea, walking for an hour with More in the garden, his arm about More's neck.

All this is Sir Thomas More, man of the world. Does not all this make him very unlike the picture of what one calls "a saint"? Can such involvement in the world be justified in terms of the Gospel? Can this be a following of Christ? Christian perfection? More's friend and instructor in Greek, Linacre, natural scientist and founder of the chairs of medicine at Oxford and Cambridge, priest as he was and holder of many ecclesiastical offices, came only late in life to open the New Testament. He happened upon the Sermon on the Mount, read the three chapters of Matthew with the utmost astonishment, and cried out: "Either this is not the Gospel, or we are not Christians." Was he not at least being consistent when he threw the book away and immersed himself once more in the study of medicine?

Living by the Gospel
But the question can be put round the other way as well: to be a true Christian, to live by the Gospel, to follow Christ, is it enough to renounce all things and forsake the world? Does a Christian, in short, need to become a monk if he is to be a saint?

What is indisputable is that it is quite possible for someone to renounce everything and live in the "state" of perfection, as given by the evangelical "counsels", and still be anything but a saint. Why?

86

Because the spirit is lacking. It was often lacking in those days. Erasmus, in his *Praise of Folly*, very clearly expressed his contempt for ignorant, immoral, unevangelical monks. The book was written in More's house and with his encouragement. Flight from the world may well be the product of weakness, inadequacy, disappointment or laziness. Flight from the world by no means necessarily means flight to God. It can be a concealed flight back to the world; the more and more worldly world of one's own ego.

But More saw the positive potentialities in monasticism too, more clearly than Erasmus, who had, as a boy, been thrust into the cloister with no inner vocation whatsoever, and who had the greatest difficulty in obtaining a dispensation from his vow of obedience. The monasteries are the only European institution of which More's Utopians explicitly approve. Indeed, More had spent four years, while a law student, sharing the religious life of the London Carthusians. It is said that at this period he also contemplated becoming a Franciscan. He saw the positive potentialities in forsaking the world as an emphatic protest against the secularization of man and an explicit making room in man's life for God. Throughout his life, he never ceased to have a certain secret nostalgia for it. But after a long and searching examination he came to the conclusion that he was not made for the monastic life, not called to forsake the world.

Did this mean that More was giving up the idea of living by the Gospel and following Christ? To

87

have a "state" of evangelical perfection without the *spirit* of evangelical perfection is not a possibility for a Christian. But could not a life in the *spirit* of evangelical perfection without the "state" be a genuine Christian possibility? What is the point of "the Gospel"? What is the good news of Jesus?

The message of Jesus is summed up in the words: "The time is accomplished, and the Kingdom of God is at hand." (Mk 1:15.) The reign of God is not yet present, but it is already breaking in. Its dawn is already manifesting itself. The appearance and work and teaching of Jesus are the sign of it. It is not men but God himself who is setting up his kingdom, his reign, by which all the sin and suffering of the world is taken away and the People of God, awaiting the fulfilment of the promises of the Prophets, is given the forgiveness of sins, the blessing of salvation:

> Blessed are ye poor;
> for yours is the Kingdom of God.
> Blessed are ye that hunger now:
> for you shall be filled.
> Blessed are ye that weep now:
> for you shall laugh. [Lk 6:20 f.]

This message summons man to a decision: "Repent and believe the gospel!" (Mk 1:15.) Jesus himself, in his own person, signifies this demand from God for a decision: "Behold more than Solomon here . . . Behold more than Jonah here." (Lk 11:31 f.) In Jesus' summons, it is the authori-

tative voice of God himself that speaks, before whom
there can be no evasion. The choice is unambiguous
and radical: God and his kingdom or the world and
its goods. Neither family nor possessions nor public
order can stand between a man and this radical
decision between God and the world. Jesus himself
forsook family, house and home. And he snatched
away a little band of men from their families, houses
and homes to go with him as his disciples. It is true
he did not urge everyone to leave his family, house
and home; Jesus was not a social revolutionary.
But this he did do: he confronted every individual,
every individual, with the radical decision of where
he is going to set his heart; on God or on the goods of
this world. Neither property nor family nor public
order must keep a man from *setting his heart solely
on God, the Lord, alone.*

Not property: "Lay not up to yourselves treasures
on earth . . . for where thy treasure is, there is thy
heart also." (Mt 6:19–21.) "No man can serve two
masters. For either he will hate the one, and love the
other: or he will sustain the one, and despise the
other. You cannot serve God and mammon." (Mt
6:24.) And how perilous is wealth: "How hardly
shall they that have riches enter into the kingdom of
God! . . . It is easier for a camel to pass through the
eye of a needle, than for a rich man to enter into the
Kingdom of God." (Mk 10:23,25.) There is a
warning against earthly cares: "Be not solicitous
therefore, saying: What shall we ear, or what shall
we drink, or wherewith shall we be clothed? For after

89

all these things do the heathens seek. For your Father knoweth that you have need of all these things. Seek ye therefore first the kingdom of God and his justice, and all these things shall be added unto you." (Mt 6:31–3.)

Not the family: "If any man come to me, and hate not his father, and mother, and wife, and children, and brethren, and sisters, yea and his own life also, he cannot be my disciple." (Lk 14:26.) "Do not think that I came to send peace upon earth: I came not to send peace, but the sword. For I came to set a man at variance against his father, and the daughter against her mother, and the daughter-in-law against her mother-in-law. And a man's enemies shall be they of his own household. He that loveth father or mother more than me, is not worthy of me; and he that loveth son or daughter more than me, is not worthy of me." (Mt 10:34–7.)

Not public law and order: "You have heard that it was said to them of old . . . But I say to you . . . !" (Mt 5:21–48.) It is not only the commandments contained in the law that bind men; it is not only homicide, adultery and perjury that are against the commandment of God, but even anger, evil desire and untruthfulness. Above and beyond every formula of law, what God demands is man's whole will. But this means that he demands the abandonment of one's rights: "But I say to you not to resist evil: but if one strike thee on thy right cheek, turn to him also the other. And if a man will contend with thee in judgment and take away thy coat, let go thy cloak also unto him. And whosoever will force thee one mile, go with him other two." (Mt 5:39–41.) This leads to the reversal of all human rank: "You know that they who seem to rule over the Gentiles, lord it over them: and their princes have power over them. But it is not so among you: but whosoever will be greater, shall be your minister. And whosoever will be first among you, shall be the servant of all." (Mk 10:42–4.)

This, then, is what is meant by following Christ "If any man will follow me, let him deny himself and take up his cross and follow me." (Mk 8:34.) It is a radical decision: "No man putting his hand to the plough and turning back, is fit for the kingdom of God." (Lk 9:62.) Thus God wants the whole of man; he wants his heart. Not so that man shall abandon the world; Jesus sent his disciples out into the world. But so that man shall be unhampered and free from the world, totally in readiness. In readiness for what? For fulfilling God's will, so as thus to be ready for the kingdom of God: "Whosoever shall do the will of God, he is my brother and my sister and mother." (Mk 3:35.) What does God's will require? Not merely a negative renunciation of the world, but a positive self-giving: love. No new commandments are formulated, no new particular requirements laid down; there is only the one completely concrete demand, which is at once quite unlimited and the answer to each individual case: " 'Thou shalt love the Lord thy God with thy whole heart, and with thy whole soul, and with thy whole mind.'

This is the greatest and the first commandment. And the second is like to this: 'Thou shalt love thy neighbour as thyself.' On these two commandments dependeth the whole Law and the Prophets." (Mt 22:37–40.) What shows Christian perfection is the love of enemies: "Love your enemies and pray for them that persecute you, that you may be the children of your Father who is in heaven, who maketh his sun to rise upon the good and bad and raineth upon the just and the unjust. . . . Be you therefore perfect, as also your heavenly Father is perfect." (Mt 5:44 f., 48.)

Who, then, is the follower of Christ, the man who is living perfectly by his Gospel? The man who free from all worldly attachment, is always in readiness; readiness for God and God's demands, which he meets every day in his neighbour, in the everyday life of the world.

Thomas More was ready day by day. He had not given his heart to the goods of this world. He remained in the world but did not let himself be bound by it. He had preserved an ultimate independence from the world, and interior freedom for God. This comes out in all kinds of small matters.

Sir Thomas More delighted in his possessions, but was not subject to them. More, the man of the world, was no *bon-vivant*. His inner superiority to the things of this world shows in his indifference in matters of appearance and of eating and drinking; he normally preferred simple fare to fine dishes. He was totally without greed or parsimony, gave freely of his wealth, and established an almshouse in Chelsea. This meant that after his resignation of the chancellorship he found himself in considerable straits. He was extremely anxious that his children, too, should be free from vanity. He tried to cure his daughter-in-law Anne Crisacre of it; when she asked him for a necklace of pearls he gave her—never at a loss for a joke—one of white peas. His inner freedom in regard to possessions comes out particularly strikingly on an occasion when, in his absence, his barns were destroyed by fire. He wrote to his wife Alice that she should compensate the neighbours to whose land the fire had spread: "For an I should not leave myself a spoon, there shall no poor neighbour of mine bear no loss by any chance happened in my house; I pray you be with my children and your household merry in God." His wife is to get a supply of corn for the household, and to decide whether they should keep the piece of land or not: "But I would not that any man were suddenly sent away, he wot ne'er whither." Thus More enjoyed his possessions, but his heart was given to God, the Lord, alone. How serious he was in his choice between God and possessions and in his radical readiness for God, the future was to show.

Sir Thomas More loved his family, but he was not wholly engrossed in the life of marriage and family. For all his delight in the atmosphere of his cultured family and in the rich community life lived in the circle of his wife and children and their numerous guests, More realized very well that this, so to say,

93

horizontal dimension of human relationship is not the ultimately decisive thing; that, in everything, what matters is to be aware of the all-important vertical dimension of relationship with God. Thus More took good care that God should not be forgotten in the everyday life of his family. Hence he established a family life of prayer according to the forms of his day, and reading of the Scriptures in common. Every evening when the master of the house was at home, the whole household assembled for prayer. On Sundays and feasts they went to church, and on great feast-days all attended midnight Mass. More himself usually got up at two in the morning, and occupied himself with study and prayer until seven. He assisted at Mass every morning. Even when the King once sent for him repeatedly and urgently, he refused to come until Mass was over; Henry VIII took it in good part. During meals, a member of the family would read a chapter of Scripture with Nicholas of Lyra's commentaries. Not till this reading had been discussed was More's household fool allowed to lead the conversation into other paths. Thus More loved his family, but his heart was given to God the Lord alone. How serious he was in his choice between God and family and in his radical readiness for God, the future was to show.

Sir Thomas More greatly respected the law and the State, but for him they were not the highest thing. More devoted himself as few have done to the law, the kingdom and his king, but he preserved an inner detachment from it all, an overriding freedom. At the news that More had been summoned by the King to Court, Erasmus said somewhat ruefully:" . . . we shall get no more news from Utopia to make us laugh", and adds: "I know that More would rather laugh than be carried in official state." In fact, More avoids the Court as much as he can, as much as other men seek it. At the beginning of his courtier's life he wrote, in good humour, to Bishop Fisher: "Everybody knows that I didn't want to come to court, and the King often twits me about it; I sit as uneasily as a clumsy rider in the saddle." It was immediately after More had been made Under-Treasurer and knighted that he wrote the most sombre of all his books, the *Four Last Things:* the task of life is to meditate on death; the world, even for one who holds power and authority, is a prison, in which each prisoner is waiting to be led away to his execution; "For if ye took the matter aright, the place a prison, yourself a prisoner condemned to death, from which ye cannot escape, ye would reckon this gear as worshipful as if a gentleman thief, when he should go to Tyburn, would leave for a memorial the arms of his ancestors painted on a post in Newgate. Surely, I suppose that . . . men would bear themselves not much higher in their hearts for any rule or authority that they bear in this world, which they may well perceive to be indeed no better but one prisoner bearing a rule among the remnant . . . or at the uttermost, one so put in trust with the gaoler that he is half an under-gaoler over his fellows, till the sheriff and the cart come for him."

Even when More had received, not just "any rule or authority" but the rule and authority of Lord Chancellor, he still remained the same simple, unaffected, humble, selfless man as before; as being, after the King, the highest in the State, and therefore the servant of all. Sir Thomas dresses simply and wears his gold chain only when it is absolutely necessary; he takes no account of outward forms and loves equality and freedom. None of his servants has ever fallen into disgrace. His faithful secretary, John Harris, has the duty of pointing out to him any mistake he may make. More is constantly ready to help anyone as a matter of course: time, money, influence with the King and in high places is at anyone's disposal. With kind and merry conversation he knows how to cheer the depressed and sorrowful. "You might call him the general patron of all who are hard up." He himself makes no demands on others. Lord Chancellor Wolsey once wrote to the King of More that "he is not the most ready to speak and solicit his own cause". And to Polydore Vergil, who thought that More felt for some reason offended with him, Erasmus wrote: "What you write about More is all nonsense; why, he does not remember even grave injuries." More was capable of loving his neighbour to the point of letting him have his cloak as well as his coat, of going the two miles with him. of turning the other cheek. Thus his respect for law and State was high, but his heart was given to God the Lord alone. How serious he was in his choice between State and God and in his radical readiness for God, the future was to show.

Henry VIII and his chancellor were both men of the world, and both wished to be Christians. Henry, who boldly proclaimed himself "sole protector and supreme head of the Church and clergy of England", appears as one who was enslaved to the world in the family, social and political spheres: sensuality, wealth and power were his idols, which he preferred before the Kingdom of God. It is not a question of judging Henry, but the difference between him and More shows clearly where the issue lies. To More, too, family, possessions and State meant much. But neither family nor wealth nor power were his idols. God alone was God for him. As man of the world, taking an honest delight in the world, Sir Thomas sought to live in the world as a Christian, living according to the Gospel as a follower of Christ. He did it unostentatiously and without fuss. Who, looking at Holbein's portrait, would guess that this man, who looks so little like a "saint" and displays the costly furs of a man of the world, has long been wearing under them a rough hair-shirt—an object of scandal, perhaps, to many people today—which severely punished him, sometimes leaving blood on his clothes, and of which only his favourite daughter, Margaret, was supposed to know anything?

More important than such details is the fact that Thomas More, in his whole life in the world, put into

D

practice those words of St Paul which express, more perhaps than any others, the situation of a Christian in the world:

> They also who have wives be as if they had none; and they that weep as though they wept not; and they that rejoice as if they rejoiced not; and they that buy as though they possessed not; and they that use this world as if they used it not. [1 Cor 7:29–31.]

This is the freedom of a Christian living "in Christ", who lets the whole of his daily life be unostentatiously determined by Christ. This is the glad freedom of a Christian, which by God's grace is given to men in this world by faith. God, who is freedom itself, makes unfree man free, in Christ.

The freedom of a Christian

Is the whole point, then, that a Christian should forsake the world and its goods? This is not the decisive thing. It is not even the normal thing. To forsake the world or any particular sphere within it is a charism of the Spirit that may well be bestowed on some particular individual, a special call from God affecting that particular individual. Thus Paul was given the charism of celibacy; an eschatological sign that the last times have begun—"The time is short" (1 Cor 7:29), "The fashion of this world passeth away" (1 Cor 7:31)—a sign visibly lifted up of the passing away of this world and the creation of the new man which has been achieved in Christ. Paul glories in the charism of celibacy, but hastens to add: "But every one hath his proper gift from God; one after this manner, and another after that." (1 Cor 7:7; cf. Mt 19:11 f.) According to Paul, it is not only these especially striking gifts that are charisms of the Spirit, but all works of brotherly love: "And having different gifts, according to the grace that is given us, either prophecy, to be used according to the rule of faith; or ministry, in ministering; or he that teacheth, in doctrine; he that exhorteth, in exhorting." (Rom 12:6–8.)

The Christian is to rejoice with them that rejoice and weep with them that weep. (Rom 12:15.) He can enjoy this world and its goods without fear or hypocrisy. Jesus himself, very different in this from the ascetic John the Baptist, took part in banquets and let himself be abused as "a glutton and a wine-drinker". (Mt 11:19.) He set a high value on marriage, reasserted its indissolubility, and was tenderly affectionate towards children. He would not interfere in property matters, and proposed no new distribution of wealth. He accepted the authority of the State and its right to levy taxes, and saw civic duties in a positive light. Nor did Jesus want to cut his disciples off from the world. He did not want them, like the Essenes, to dissociate themselves from the people and found closed communities with a strict moral code. Nor did he want them to form closed groups within the general community of the people. He sent his disciples out into the world. Peter, the brothers of the Lord and the other apostles took their wives with them when they went to preach the Gospel. (1 Cor 9:5.)

Many different ways lie open for Christian "perfection", the perfect striving of a Christian existence towards God. The decisive thing for a Christian is not that he surrenders the goods of this world but that he does not surrender himself to them, does not give himself away to them, does not lose himself in them: neither in sex nor in wealth nor in power. A Christian can only surrender and give himself away to God, only lose himself in him, whom he has chosen, fundamentally and radically, in faith; God alone is absolute, all else is relative. Thus the decisive thing for a Christian is not that he abandons this world and its goods but that he does not become enslaved to them. Putting it positively, that he preserves the glorious *freedom* of a Christian in respect of the world, a freedom which shows itself by interior *detachment* from the things of this world. The decisive thing is not an external, spatial detachment but an interior, personal one. Paul does not reject the "abundance" of this world; he knows how to live with it. But he preserves the over-riding detachment of a free man, which makes him, in the last analysis, *indifferent* to abundance and to want: "I have learned, in whatsoever state I am, to be content therewith. I know both how to be brought low, and I know to abound (everywhere and in all things I am instructed): both to be full and to be hungry; both to abound and

49106

suffer need. I can do all things in him who strengthen-
eth me." (Phil 4:11–13.) Such is the true, cheerful
attitude of a Christian in the world; not the twisted
rigidity of "having to sacrifice oneself" but what
Paul calls "autarchy": sufficiency, freedom, in *any*
situation.

A man enjoying this freedom is free from the
anxiety of a man who is subject to the world, who
lives under the "spirit of bondage" which necessarily
leads to "fear". (Rom 8:15) A man who is a slave to
the world is "solicitous"; "he is solicitous for the
things of the world" (1 Cor 7:33), as though he could
thus ensure himself a future. A man who is a slave
of the world "covets"; he "covets evil things" (1
Cor 10:6), as though he could find rest and peace
in the "works of the flesh". A man who is a slave to
the world "glories in himself": he "glories" in his
own strength and achievements and works (1 Cor
4:7) as though he had something which he had not
received. A man who is a slave to the world "trusts
in the flesh"; he "trusts in himself" (2 Cor 1:9),
as though he could find stability in himself. This
man, who has become enslaved to the world and its
goods, who lives not only "in the flesh" but "according to the flesh" is involved in error; indeed, in sin.
Instead of to the Creator of the world, he is handing
himself over to the created world, seeking, in vain,
to find in it the norm and the strength for his life;
he thus falls into "enmity with God". (Rom 8:7.)

But the Christian, who is not a slave to the world,
but, free as regards the world, is a servant or rather

a child of God, is solicitous not for the things of the world but "for the things that belong to the Lord" (1 Cor 7:32), and thus, in fact, for "nothing". (Phil 4:6.) His desire is not for the works of the flesh but "to be with Christ". (Phil 1:23.) He glories not in anything of his own but "in the Lord" (2 Cor 10:17), and hence in his own "infirmity". (2 Cor 11:30.) He trusts, not in himself but "in God who raiseth the dead". (2 Cor 1:9.) The Christian in the world is "not his own" (1 Cor 6:19), he belongs to God. He lives "not according to the flesh, but according to the spirit" (Rom 8:4); he clings not to what is visible, transitory and dying but to the invisible, to the eternal, to life. He lives thus not for himself but for God, in "the freedom wherewith Christ has made us free". (Gal 5:1.) This freedom does not consist in unrestrained, arbitrary wilfulness but in a new, joyful service of God and one's neighbour. Freedom implies a demand on us: "Be not conformed to this world: but be reformed in the newness of your mind, that you may prove what is the good and the acceptable and the perfect will of God." (Rom 12:2.)

Thus the Christian takes to himself the great saying, "All things are lawful to me." (1 Cor 16:12.) But, "I will not be brought under the power of any." (1 Cor 6:12.) There is in this world, indeed, "nothing that is unclean of itself" (Rom 14:14), neither in the family, the social nor the political sphere, neither sex nor property nor power. But it is possible for me to lose my freedom to something in the world, to let myself be dominated by it, so that it becomes for me an idol. Then we come up against the words, "All things are lawful to me, but all things are not expedient." (1 Cor 6:12.) Moreover, it is possible that what is in itself lawful to me, and even expedient for me, may do damage to my neighbour. And then the words that apply are "All things are lawful for me, but all things do not edify. Let no man seek his own, but that which is another's." (1 Cor 10:23–4.)

A Christian is at the service of others (1 Cor 9:19), but in freedom: "Be not made the bond-slaves of men." (1 Cor 7:23.) A Christian is not ultimately bound by any opinions, judgments, assessments of value, conventions or traditions of men: "For why is my liberty judged by another man's conscience?" (1 Cor 10:29.) My own conscience, in its awareness of good and evil, is what binds me. (1 Cor 8:7–12; 10:25–30.)

The freedom of a Christian is freedom in the world, freedom from the world for God alone, in loving service of his neighbour: in the family, the social and the political spheres. This freedom is *always* demanded of a Christian in his enjoyment of the world, *always* required of one who "uses this world". (1 Cor 7:31.) He must never lose himself in the temptation of desiring to enjoy, to possess, to dominate; never surrender to the demon of *eros* or of mammon or of power. He can love his wife and family, enjoy his possessions, act in the order of politics and law—all in freedom. But at any moment, this fundamental freedom of the Christian who uses this world may—for God, in the service of his neighbour—take on the form of *renunciation*. In renouncing the goods of this world the Christian is not renouncing his freedom. On the contrary, renunciation is what calls most fully upon his freedom and brings it into play to the maximum extent; this is how far I can go as a Christian, even to the point of free renunciation! It is when this maximum call is made on it that a Christian's freedom is *put to the test*. In renunciation, *here-and-now* renunciation, he shows of what quality his freedom has been, *everywhere and at all times*.

But the *great* test of a Christian's freedom arises when he is faced with the choice of abandoning not just something but *everything* for the sake of God and his kingdom: of giving away "all that he has" to possess the field with the hidden treasure, the pearl of great price. (Mt 13:44–6.) The great test of a Christian's freedom arises when what is demanded of him is readiness not merely for some sort of renunciation but for *total* renunciation. It was with this great test of freedom that Sir Thomas More was faced.

Death and Life

For a Christian who has radically chosen God and his kingdom in faith, so as to be ready for anything, this great test does not represent a break but a continuous advance in faith. For Thomas More, the great test did not involve a conversion but a further putting into practice of that radical readiness in faith which he had maintained, in principle, through all his years as a student, lawyer, judge, diplomat and Lord Chancellor; readiness for anything, for any sacrifice. That fundamental readiness was now required to meet the fullest demands.

"*Indignatio principis mors est*, the wrath of the prince is death", said the Duke of Norfolk to More. "Is that all, my Lord?" was More's answer. "Then in good faith is there no more difference between your Grace and me, but that I shall die today and you tomorrow."

Thomas More could not follow a Henry VIII who, in pursuit of his matrimonial affairs, had declared himself, over and against the Pope, as "sole protector and supreme head of the Church and clergy of England". He tried to avoid the conflict and withdrew into private life; he tendered his resignation on "grounds of health". He did not seek martyrdom. He constantly insisted that he respected the consciences of those who thought differently from himself and would not try to dissuade them from their position. He said that he did not set himself up to judge the conscience, the loyalty or the wisdom of other men, but was only concerned with himself and what his own conscience commanded, adding that that same conscience brought to his mind so many imperfections of his past life that he could only implore God for mercy. But the freedom which he allowed to others was not granted to himself; he was accused of high treason.

It is not our business here to assess the justification for More's deciding against Henry. More was certainly no papal absolutist, no divinizer of the Papacy: "The Pope is a prince as you are. It may hereafter so fall out that Your Grace and he may vary upon some points, whereupon may grow breach of amity between you both." Such was his warning to Henry when the latter, in the first part of his reign, exaggerated the papal authority even in temporal matters. But More was equally certainly no royal absolutist, no divinizer of the monarchy: "And forasmuch as this indictment is grounded upon an Act of Parliament directly repugnant to the laws of God and his holy Church, the supreme government of which, or of any part whereof, may no temporal prince presume by any law to take upon him, as rightfully belonging to the See of Rome . . . it is therefore in law, amongst Christian men insufficient to charge any Christian man." Such were his words to the court that tried him, when Henry, in the second part of his reign, was setting aside the authority of the Pope in spiritual things. Whatever one's opinion is of More's decision, one cannot but respect it; it was the honourable decision, in conscience, of a believing Christian, who was ready to pay any price whatever for it: "Very and pure necessity, for the discharge of my conscience, enforceth me to speak so much. Wherein I call and appeal to God, whose only sight pierceth into the very depth of man's heart, to be my witness."

Now, when More's fundamental choice between

God and the world is subjected to the ultimate test, this man of the world resolutely gives up *everything* for the known will of God.

He renounces his position in the State; he resigns office, and gives back the Great Seal to the King. The man who was England's chief statesman is thrown into the Tower.

He renounces his possessions; he loses his income, dismisses those in his service, submits to the confiscation of his goods. Poor, prematurely aged, and ill, leaning on a stick, the ex-Lord Chancellor faces his judges.

He renounces his family: he says farewell to his wife and children, who were eventually refused permission even to visit him in prison. Complete loneliness has come upon the man who signs his farewell letter to his Italian friend Antonio Bonvisi: "Thomas More: I should in vain put to it, 'Yours', for thereof can you not be ignorant, since you have bought it with so many benefits. Nor now I am not such a one that it forceth [= matters] whose I am."

The following of Christ had become a literal reality for Thomas More. He wrote in prison: "Now to this great glory can there no man come headless. Our head is Christ: and therefore to him must we be joined, and as members of his must we follow him, if we will come thither. He is our guide to guide us thither. . . . Knew you not that Christ must suffer passion, and by that way enter into his kingdom? Who can for very shame desire to enter into the

Kingdom of Christ with ease, when himself entered
not into his own without pain?"

He drew his strength from the passion of Christ.
He prepared for his end by writing a *Treatise on the
Passion*. When he came to the words "they laid hands
on him", his books and papers and everything he
had with him in prison were taken from him. He
had before been deprived for a time of writing
materials, and had written a letter with a piece of
charcoal:" . . . Of worldly things I no more desire
than I have . . . Written with a coal by your tender
loving father, who in his poor prayers forgotteth none
of you all . . . And thus fare ye heartily well for lack
of paper. Our Lord keep me continually true,
faithful and plain."

And thus Sir Thomas More died as few have died
before him or since; on the scaffold, cheerfully, with
a smile, in the royal freedom of a Christian man.
He prayed briefly for God's mercy, embraced the
executioner, who begged his forgiveness, confessed
his Catholic faith and called on all present to pray
for the King, saying that he died "the King's good
servant, but God's first". His last words were a joke
about his beard, which he arranged on the block so
that it should not be cut, since his beard at least
had committed no treason.

Thomas More lost his life to save it. In him, the
paradox of Christian living was visibly fulfilled:

We are reviled, and we bless:
we are persecuted, and we suffer it.

We are blasphemed, and we entreat.
  [1 Cor 4:12 f.]

As deceivers, and yet true:
as unknown, and yet known:
as dying, and behold we live:
as chastised, and not killed:
as sorrowful, yet always rejoicing:
as needy, yet enriching many:
as having nothing, and possessing all things.
  [2 Cor 6:8–10.]

Thomas More, in his secular dress, with his secular culture, in the midst of his family, his possessions, and his public life, was a saint. Not because he was without faults and sins; he had them, like every other human being, and he confessed them often before his death: "I have not been a man of such holy living as I might be bold to offer myself to death, and therefore put myself not forward, but drew back, lest God for my presumption might suffer me to fall. Howbeit, if God draw me to it himself, then trust I in his great mercy that he shall not fail to give me grace and strength." But, with all his sinfulness, he was a saint, because he, as a sinful man, chosen out and embraced by God's grace in Christ—"sanctified in Christ Jesus, called to be a saint" (1 Cor 1:2)—made a radical choice of God, kept himself ready for God throughout his whole life in the world, and finally underwent the supreme test of that readiness in his death. Thus he knew the love of God in Christ,

from which nothing can separate a man, neither life
nor death:

> All things are yours . . . ,
> whether the world, or life, or death,
> or things present, or things to come:
> for all are yours;
> and you are Christ's:
> and Christ is God's. [1 Cor 3:22–3.]

The example set before a Christian is such that it is
possible for him, as a Christian, chosen out and
embraced by God's grace in Christ, to live by the
Gospel in the world; to follow Christ in the world,
in the midst of his family and his possessions and the
State; to live soberly, unsentimentally, honestly,
unfanatically, unpietistically, seriously and at the
same time joyfully: a holy life. What, then, is the
real point for a Christian in the world? To make a
radical choice in faith, despite all our sinfulness,
and to sustain it through ordinary daily life, for God
the Lord and his kingdom. To keep, in the world,
one's fundamental freedom from the world, in the
midst of one's family, one's possessions and the
State, in service of God and of one's brothers. To
be cheerfully ready at any time to embody this
freedom in renunciation, even, when called on for it,
in total renunciation. It is only in this freedom from
the world, in the world, for God the Lord, given by
God's grace, that the Christian can find strength,
consolation, power, joy—victory.

4. Truthfulness as a Demand of the Message of Jesus

"Christ Jesus, 'though he was by nature God . . . emptied himself, taking the nature of a slave' (Phil 2:6), and 'being rich, he became poor' (2 Cor 8:9) for our sakes. Thus, although the Church needs human resources to carry out its mission, it is not established to seek earthly glory, but to proclaim humility and self-sacrifice, even by its own example. . . . The Church, embracing sinners in its bosom, is at the same time holy and always in need of being purified, and incessantly pursues the path of penance and renewal."—*Dogmatic Constitution on the Church*, I, 8.

I

What did *Jesus* want? Jesus proclaimed the kingdom of God, which was near, which had even begun. Man must commit himself radically to God and his kingdom; must fulfil the will of God uncompromisingly in total love; must, because he is completely at the disposal of God, be at the disposal of his fellow man. In radical commitment to God, radical commitment of fellow men. That was the message of Jesus, and it soon brought him a host of enemies. By its very demand for a true human existence before God, it was a passionate protest against human dishonesty: a protest against the legalism of that man whose final norm is not the will of God and love, but an external law, a commandment; a protest against the feigned piety of a spiritless literalism and against an empty ritualism, not in accord with the inner reality of the heart, striving for a merely external correctness rather than for the true and the genuine. Against this dishonesty, the Gospel (Mt 15:8 f.; Mk 7:6 f.) quotes Isaiah (29:13), "This people pays me lip-service, but their heart is far from me: their worship of me is in vain, for they teach as doctrines the commandments of men." What Christian could be so naïve as to think that all this only applies to the Jews? Jesus' protest is not merely against falsehood in the sense of a casuistic moral theology, but against everything which the gospels call "hypocrisy". The Greek word employed, *hypokrisis*, comes from *hypokrinesthai*. This is a familiar term of Greek theatre and means "to play a role". The verb is used for all play-acting, all hypocritical shame which, disguising its true nature and intentions, only appears masked: from God, from men, from itself.

Jesus rebuked his contemporaries for this sham and hypocrisy—hypocrisy, as described in the sermon on the mount (Mt 6:5–8,14,16–18), in almsgiving, at prayer, in fasting. Hypocrisy, however, also in a dishonest casuistry: in connection with the Sabbath, for example, where Jesus must call attention to the obvious truth that the laws were made for the sake of man and not man for the laws (cf. Mk 2:27). According to Jesus, prostitutes and publicans who are honest with themselves come off better than the so-called righteous. In contradiction to all dishonest legalism and pietism, love alone is of final importance to Jesus: "Is it permitted to do good or to do evil on the sabbath, to save life or to kill?" (Mk 3:4).

Can one imagine a sharper judgment on all dishonesty, falseness and hypocrisy than the great lamentation of Matthew 23, with its refrain, "you hypocrites": "Alas for you, lawyers and Pharisees,

114

hypocrites! You clean the outside of cup and dish, which you have filled inside by robbery and self-indulgence! Blind Pharisee! Clean the inside of the cup first; then the outside will be clean also. Alas for you, lawyers and Pharisees, hypocrites! You are like tombs covered with whitewash; they look well from outside, but inside they are full of dead men's bones and all kinds of filth. So it is with you: outside you look like honest men, but inside you are brim-full of hypocrisy and crime" (Mt 23:25–28). How encouraging, however, for the truthful, honest and sincere man is the word, "The lamp of the body is the eye. If your eyes are sound, you will have light for your whole body; if the eyes are bad, your whole body will be in darkness." (Mt 6:22 f. and parallels.)

II

But if we want to see what the message of Jesus means for the truthfulness of the Church, then we must not merely cite the statements of Jesus in the synoptic tradition against hypocrisy, but rather—as already indicated at the beginning of this section—start out from the *centre of Jesus' message*. In its proclamation of Jesus as the Christ, the Lord, the Church does indeed appeal at the same time to the message of Jesus itself. But this message of Jesus itself has for its theme, not the Church, but the reign of God. And this message of Jesus about God's reign poses the fundamental question of truthfulness for every church which appeals to the message of Jesus. Compared to this fundamental question of the truthfulness of the Church, all other questions about the "institutional" factors are secondary. Here the Church in its whole existence is involved and challenged. We shall try therefore to give concrete expression to this basic critical question from five aspects.

a. A truthful church, according to Jesus' message, is a *provisional* church. Jesus proclaimed the reign of God as a decisively *future, end-time, final* event.

Question: Has the Church remained faithful to this message? Does it regard itself really only as a provisional church? More concretely: may a truthful church in this end-time ever place itself at the centre of its preaching? Must it not, arising as it does from the reign of God fulfilled in Christ, constantly point beyond itself to the reign of God which it awaits as the critical fulfilment of its mission? Is it not for the first time approaching not merely the particular, but the universal, not merely the transitory, but the definitive revelation of God's conquering glory? May it then ever set itself up as an end in itself, as if it could ever be a glory flourishing and complete in itself? As if men's decision were centred primarily not on God, not on Jesus the Christ, but on the Church. As if it were the end and fulfilment of world-history, as if it were the definitive reality.

Is not a church which forgets in this end-time that it is something temporary, provisional, transitional, faced with excessive demands on its truthfulness? Must it not tire, relax its effort and break down, because it has no future? Is not that church alone able to maintain its truthfulness which always remembers that it will find its goal, not in itself, but in God's kingdom? Because it thus knows that too much is not required of it, that it does not need to provide anything at all final, to offer any lasting home, that it must not be at all surprised if—in its provisional nature—it is shaken with doubts, blocked by hindrances and oppressed by cares? Does then the Church today really see itself in this way? So far as it can do so, it is a truthful church.

b. According to the message of Jesus a truthful church means an unassuming church: Jesus proclaimed the reign of God as *a mighty deed of God himself*.

Question: Has the Church remained faithful to this message? Does this church really see itself as an unassuming church? More concretely: may a truthful church in this end-time, while making the utmost exertions in the service of God's reign, ever want to create God's kingdom itself? As if God does not create it *for* the Church! As if it had to place its whole trust, not in his, but in its own action. Can the Church in this end-time do more than pray for God's reign, seek it, intensively prepare itself and the world by action and suffering for God's reign? May it ever glorify itself and boast before God and men of its own vital and formative power? May it ever raise claims against God by her resolutions, regulations and ideas, instead of defending God's claim in the world? Could it ever distrust the grace of God in its ecclesiastical know-all and be intent upon its own home-made sovereignty and greatness? May it ever suppose that in fact it bestows grace itself, instead of being constantly in need of it?

Would not a church be bound to become untruthful if it imagined that *it* creates what is decisive in this end-time, that it has to bring about, build up, erect the kingdom of God from its own resources and achievement? Would it not thus be bound to scatter and destroy, since it would lack the selfless faith which trusts wholly in God's decisive deed? Is it not that church alone which is convinced in trusting faith that God inaugurates, sustains and rules this end-time and that he will bestow the new, finished reality of the world and of men: is it not that church alone which can be truthful and thus gather and build up, because power is granted to its humble trust? Since the Church then knows that, with all its efforts, what ultimately counts is not *its* theories and practices, that it is not its own catalogue of achievement and brilliant statistics which guarantee the coming of the kingdom of God and hence that no want of an echo may prevent it from continuing to call, no failure dishearten it. Does then the Church today really see itself in this way? As far as it can do so, it is a truthful church.

c. According to the message of Jesus, a truthful church means a *ministering* church. Jesus preached the reign of God as a *purely religious* reign.

Truthfulness as a Demand of the Message of Jesus

Question: Has the Church remained faithful to this message? Does this church really see itself as a *ministering* church? More concretely: may a truthful church in this end-time ever act like a religious-political theocracy? Is its character not that of a spiritual *diakonia*? Instead of setting up an empire of spiritual–unspiritual power, has it not been given the grace of ministry in the form of a servant: service of God as service of men and service of men as service of God? How could it then in this end-time ever have recourse to the methods of secular seizure and establishment of power, of political strategy and intrigue? How could it radiate worldly glory and splendour, how assign places of honour to right and left, how hand out titles and distinctions of worldly dignity? How could it want to hoard the goods of this world, money and gold, to keep more than is necessary? How could it get mixed up with the powers of this world, how simply identify itself with any sort of worldly grouping, a political party, a cultural association, an economic and social power-group? How commit itself uncritically and unconditionally to a particular economic, social, cultural, political, philosophical or ideological system? How could it fail constantly to disturb, estrange, and question these worldly powers and systems with its revolutionary message and precisely on account of this have to face their resistance and attack? How could it avoid suffering, contempt, calumny, persecution?

Does a church which in this end-time overlooks the fact that it exists for selfless service to men, to enemies, to the world, not lose its truthfulness and thus also its dignity, its validity, its reason for existing, because it abandons the true imitation of Christ? Conversely does not the Church alone which remains aware of the fact that it is not itself, but God's reign, which will come "in power and glory", does not this church alone find its true greatness and thus its truthful existence only in being small? Because it then knows that it is great precisely without the show of power and splendour, that it can rely upon the agreement and support of the mighty ones of this world only very conditionally and to a limited extent, that its existence is constantly ignored, neglected and merely tolerated by the world or even regretted, deplored and wished away, that its activity is constantly ridiculed, suspected, disapproved of and hindered, that for it nevertheless above all other dominations God's reign is unassailable. Does the Church today really see itself in this way? As far as it can do so, it is a truthful church.

d. According to the message of Jesus, a truthful church is a church *conscious of guilt*. Jesus proclaimed the reign of God as a saving event for *sinners*.

Question: Has the Church remained faithful to this message? Does this church really see itself as a church *conscious of guilt*? More concretely: may a truthful church in this end-time—for all its opposition to the world and its powers—ever behave as a threatening, intimidating institution, preaching doom and creating fear? May it announce to the world tidings of doom instead of the message of salvation, threatening words instead of the message of joy, a declaration of war instead of the message of peace? The Church exists in fact not for the pious and just, but for the unjust and the impious. It should in fact not condemn and anathematize, but—for all the seriousness of its message—heal, pardon and save. Even its often unavoidable admonitions should in fact never be ends in themselves, but pointers to God's offer of grace. Nor can it—even with all the proofs of grace reaching it and precisely because of these proofs—in fact ever give itself airs as a self-righteous caste or class of the pure and holy.

Will not a church which in this end-time does not want to know that it exists as composed of sinful men for sinful men, not become hard-hearted, self-righteous, merciless and thus untruthful? Does it thus still deserve God's mercy and men's trust? Is this truthfulness, holiness and justice which it cannot itself produce not a gift of grace solely to that church which takes seriously the fact that only the consummated reign of God will have wheat and tares, good and rotten fish, separated from one another? Since such a church then knows that it does not need to adopt a high moral tone in the world, as if with it everything were ordered for the best, that it carries its treasures in very earthen vessels, that its lights are faint and flickering, its faith weak, its knowledge obscure and its confession halting, that there is not a single sin or lapse which cannot become a temptation to it and to which it is

121

not already exposed in one way or another that—for all its constant dissociation from sin—it can never have an excuse for dissociating itself from sinners. Does the Church then today really see itself in this way? As far as it can do so, it is a truthful church.

e. According to the message of Jesus, a truthful church is an *obedient* church. Jesus demanded for the reign of God *man's radical decision for God.*

Question: Has the Church remained faithful to this message? Does the Church really see itself as an *obedient* church? Is not the truthful church—and particularly as such—also faced with the choice: God and his reign or the world and its reign? Must not the Church allow nothing to hold it back from a radical decision for God? Must not it constantly turn to metanoia, away from the wickedness of the world, and submit itself to the coming reign of God, so that from this position it can turn in love to the world and to men: not therefore in ascetic separation from the world, but in radical loving obedience to God's will in the ordinary affairs of the world; not in flight from the world, but in working on the world?

Can the Church ever be allowed to avoid this radical obedience to God's will? As if perhaps the demands of the gospel held only for the "wicked world" and not also for the constantly resecularized church. As if the Church could discharge its obligation of obedience to God's holy will by obedience to itself. As if it could issue its own liturgical, dogmatic and juridical laws and regulations, traditions and customs as commandments of God; as if it could place them above or even alongside God's will as it became known in Jesus Christ. As if it could declare as eternal laws what are always time-conditioned arrangements and which can then be adapted to the ever-recurring present only with the aid of artificial and twisted interpretation.

Does not a church place itself in chains, does it not enslave itself, does it not become untruthful, if it forgets in this present age whom it has to obey, if it seizes dominion for itself, makes itself sovereign, sets itself up as lord and master. Conversely, does not that church alone become truthful and free which —for all its failures—is constantly intent upon God's reign and remembers to whom it belongs, for whom it has to decide, for whom it must constantly decide afresh without compromise and without reserve? Does not such an obedient church become truly free to imitate Christ's ministry to the world; free for the service of God in which it serves men; free for the service of men in which it serves God; free to overcome the body, sin and death, through the cross of the risen one; free for the all-embracing creative love which changes and renews the world; free for an unshakable active hope for the coming kingdom of God of complete justice, of eternal life, of true freedom and of cosmic peace, for the final reconciliation of mankind with God and the removal of all impiety? Does the Church then today really see itself in this way? As far as it can do so, it is a truthful church.

III

This is what Jesus' message means for the Church and its truthfulness. We were merely raising questions, we were raising them as members of this church and precisely *in* the church we have more right than we would have outside it to raise these questions openly and honestly. Questions which undoubtedly are also indictments. Questions which undoubtedly are not merely indictments. This is precisely what is so difficult about these questions; they cannot simply be answered with a smooth "yes" or "no". The reality of the Church as such is too complex for this, too manifold, too much light and shade, nature and un-nature. In theological terms: the concrete Church is the Church of God and at the same time—with all its institutions and constitutions—the Church of men, of sinful men constantly betraying the gospel afresh; it is the at same time in every individual member and in every one of its institutions both truthful and untruthful church, but not each as balanced off against the other or in the same way.

In Jesus Christ—who as Jesus preaching has now become through his death and his new life in God the Christ who is preached and has this made possible the whole new reality of the Church—this holds: untruthfulness is the Church's past; truthfulness its future. Each is present in its own way: the past as past, as the old; the future as future, as the new. The past of untruthfulness has no longer a future for the Church at present, but it still remains the

124

Church's past. The Church has been rescued from untruthfulness, but it still remains under attack. The Church therefore must constantly turn away again from its past towards its future, which is its truthfulness. This future by God's grace is already bestowed on it as a pledge; the Church is wholly and entirely determined by it. But it must constantly seize it afresh, have it given to it. Because the Church is truthful, it ought to be truthful: the indicative demands the imperative. This is what the apostolic preaching requires.

The New Testament is concerned with the idea of truth at every turn; it is one of the basic concepts of the New Testament. Reflecting the sense of the Old Testament word *emet*, the Greek word *alētheia*, truth, is used in the New Testament to mean that which is certain and valid, the binding norm, in other words, that on which one may rely. In the New Testament, "truth" also has the Greek meaning of conclusive evidence, manifest reality, and, consequently, the correct doctrine. St Paul simply calls his entire apostolic activity "declaring the truth openly" (2 Cor 4:2). The preaching of the gospel can be called "the message of the truth" (2 Cor 6:7; Col 1:5; Eph 1:13). The Christian faith is "obedience to the truth" (1 Pet 1:22; cf. Gal 5:7).

But it is St John who has given the word "truth" its deepest meaning. For him, it is the opposite of falsehood. Falsehood is, however, not understood in the casuistic sense, but rather designates the essence of that human world, given over to death, removed

125

from God, which, shutting itself off from the light, tries to set itself free from its creator and falls into the abyss of self-deception.

Jesus, however, came into the world as the light, in order to witness to the truth (Jn 18:37); grace and truth came through him (1:17) and the knowledge of the truth is promised to those who believe in him (8:32). The word that Jesus brings is truth (17:17), yes, he is himself the truth (14:16). By "truth" John never means a simple statement, or a teaching, not even reality in opposition to deception. He means, rather, that reality which is the only genuinely true reality: the reality proper to God. This truth "speaks", reveals Jesus (8:45), his Spirit leads one into this truth (16:13), not simply into a new teaching or doctrine or theology about God, in the newly evident reality of God, as it reveals itself in Jesus (14:9–11). This is the truth which sets us free (8:32). A new existence, a new life, a new birth of man "out of God", springing from this truth, this reality of God himself is actually possible.

The language of the New Testament is rich in examples of the interrelation of truth and truthfulness: the common Greek word *alētheia*, as well as the Old Testament word *emet*, means both truth and truthfulness: that which may be relied upon, dependability, sincerity (cf. 2 Cor 7:14; 11:10; 1 Cor 5:8; Phil 1:18; 1 Tim 2:7). In the same way, the related adjectives *alēthēs* (cf. Mk 12:14; 2 Cor 6:8; Rom 3:4; Jn 3:33; 7:18; 8:26) and *alēthinos* mean both "true" and "truthful". Truthfulness is so much taken for granted that it receives little attention in the paranese (cf. Mt 5:37; Eph 4:15; 22–25; Phil 4:8). However, the New Testament condemns almost no other sin as vehemently as hypocrisy (cf. Mt 6:1–17; 15:7 ff.; 23; Acts 5:1–11; 1 Tim 4:1 f). We hardly need to be reminded that Paul opposed Peter to his face because he had "played it false" and his conduct "did not square with the truth of the gospel" (cf. Gal 2:11–14). Significant in this regard is the weight which the New Testament places upon the *parrhēsia* (originally meaning the right to speak of everything): that is, upon candour before God and man, not obscuring or hushing up anything, unembarrassedly frank, utterly fearless.

In contrast to textbook theology, a close relationship between truth and truthfulness is found not only in the biblical view but also in that of the modern world. We can see once again that there is no fundamental contradiction between the view of the modern world which looks to the future and that of the original biblical message which looks to the past, or between *aggiornamento* and reform; we can see once again that it is not the original biblical message itself, but, rather the ecclesiastical innovations of the eleventh, thirteenth, sixteenth or nineteenth centuries which no longer matter to the modern world, which are—with some justice—reckoned as belonging to the *ancient régime*. In the final analysis, also the modern world does not care, as far as the human-personal sphere is concerned, for abstract, purely "objective" truths. Truth, for the modern world, does not simply consist in the intellect's abstract and neutral conformity with the object (*adaequatio intellectus et rei*). Finally, only those truths which are apprehended, realized and lived existentially are relevant for the modern world. Engagement is demanded, the unconditional, unreserved commitment to the truth; not the unconcerned, theorizing attitude of the mere observer. "The only thing that counts is total commitment." (J.–P. Sartre).

In this way, also, for the modern world, truth is bound up with man's personal existence, that is, with his truthfulness. Veracity is the *conditio sine qua non* of truth. Only in truthfulness is the truth of the person revealed. Only the honest man is disposed to apprehend the truth which sustains him. The full truth is closed to those who are dishonest with themselves. In this sense truthfulness is much more basic than truth itself. Even those who cannot agree on the truth must, nevertheless, agree on truthfulness. Honesty makes dialogue possible. For those living in a pluralistic society, it is not truth but honesty, truthfulness, which is the basis of all tolerance and of all social life and co-operation. Thus does honesty become a basic ethical demand, touching everyone and everything concerning man's relationship to himself, to society and to God.